IB PHYSICS
Internal Assessment
For the International Baccalaureate Diploma

Zouev Elite Publishing

This book is printed on acid-free paper.

Copyright © 2020 Zouev Elite Publishing. All rights reserved.

No part of this book may be used or reproduced in any manner whatsoever without written permission, except in the case of brief quotations embodied in critical articles or reviews.

Published 2020

Printed by Zouev Elite Publishing

ISBN 978-1-9996115-1-4, paperback.

TABLE OF CONTENTS

PART I: THE IB PHYSICS IA GUIDE 9
   1. GENERAL INTRODUCTION 10
   2. HOW TO FIND AN INTERESTING TOPIC 11
   3. BREAKDOWN OF THE GRADING MATRIX 12
   4. INTEGRATING WITH YOUR STUDIES AND THE SYLLABUS 20
   5. USEFUL RESOURCES AND LINKS 26
   6. IA CHECKLIST 27

PART II: SEVEN EXAMPLES OF EXCELLENT INTERNAL ASSESSMENT 29
   1. THE RELATIONSHIP BETWEEN SURFACE AREA AND DRAG 31
   2. INVESTIGATING TENSION, FREQUENCY, MASS PER UNIT LENGTH & WAVE VELOCITY OF A STRING USING A SONOMETER 45
   4. THE RELATIONSHIP BETWEEN TEMPERATURE AND COEFFICIENT OF RESTITUTION 67
   5. HOW DOES THE MASS OF THE COUNTERWEIGHT USED TO LAUNCH THE PROJECTILE OF FIXED MASS AFFECT THE RANGE OF THE PROJECTILE? 81
   6. STANDING WAVES AND THE EFFECT OF TEMPERATURE ON THE CLARINET 97
   7. IS IT MORE ENERGY EFFICIENT TO USE A SMALL PERSONAL FAN OR A LARGER, MULTI-PERSON FAN, FOR PERSONAL COOLING IN A HOT CLIMATE? 115

PART I
THE IB PHYSICS IA GUIDE

1. GENERAL INTRODUCTION

The Internal Assessment (IA) is an important part of your Physics IB course. Not only does it count as 20 % of your final grade (!), but it is also an **opportunity** for you to explore some physics-related concepts that you found interesting during your classes.

The Physics IA gives you a chance to experience what being a scientist really entails: asking questions and designing experiments that try to answer them. This is at the root of the scientific method! What moderators look for in a Physics IA are signs of an inquisitive mind and evidence of the student's ability to conduct an accurate experiment while making pertinent conclusions.

An inquisitive mind means that you ask yourself about the **relationship** between two different variables and are able to design an experiment to **test** what that relationship is. For the experiment to be relevant, you need to make sure that your procedure is precise and accurate, and that you are able to handle errors well. Finally, you should be able to consider the **limitations** of your experiment when you discuss your conclusions.

> **Remember:** There is nothing wrong if your experiment does not work out – the important thing is that you are **critical** about your findings, being able to explain why it did or did not work.

The Physics IA is very similar to what a "lab report" would be at university and consequently, the **formatting** and the rigour when **handling errors** are a very important part of it. In order to improve your presentation, you might want to use LaTeX but word will work too.

It does not matter which graphing software you use but you need to make sure you are comfortable adding errors and lines of best fit to your plots. Some suggestions for the software you might use are:

Presentation	Software
Typesetter	Word, Pages, LaTeX
Graphs	Excel, CurveExpert, OriginLab, LoggerPro
Plots	Desmos, Geogebra
Data Analysis	Audacity (sound), Logger Pro (motion)

There is no word limit in your IA but keep it between 6-12 pages (not including bibliography or appendices). Any additional data tables or graphs which are not essential to understand your work should be included in the appendices.

> The IA is **internally assessed** so make sure you check with your teacher if there is any format and page limit that he/she would prefer you to follow.

Use your laboratory time as an **opportunity** to develop the skills you will need to use when carrying out your IA. Finally, keep in mind that completing a great IA would also help you with the data analysis questions in **Paper 3**!

2. HOW TO FIND AN INTERESTING TOPIC

Now you know what to do, you might be wondering "how do I pick the right topic?". Start thinking about the things you are **interested in** (e.g, music, sports, etc), and make a list of the topics you found the most interesting from the Physics syllabus. Next, do a bit of research about those topics and pick a law that **relates two variables in a simple way**. If you do not find a specific law, try to see if you can explain what the relationship between the variables should be and why.

> **The simpler the better:** It is not about making a crucial finding but rather about being able to conduct an accurate and precise experiment while processing your data and interpreting your results correctly.

The most important thing is that the relationship you are studying is **crystal clear** and of some physical relevance. Therefore, you should put a lot of thought when choosing the **variables** that you will be studying. Let's recall few important things about physical variables: An experiment has a **dependent, independent** and **controlled** variables:

Variable	Explanation
Independent	The variable you change in a controlled fashion
Dependent	The variable that it is affected by the change in the independent variable
Controlled	Every other physical quantity that can alter the outcome of the experiment

When deciding on your IA topic, you should pick something **concrete, realistic** and of **interest** to you. Ideally, you want to go a bit beyond your syllabus to show **curiosity, initiative or independent thinking**. For example, if you learned about refractive index and Snell's law in class, you might want to study how the **refractive index (dependent)** of a material changes with its **temperature (independent)**.

> **Keep in mind:** The dependent or independent variable might not be the things that you measure, but rather **what you calculate with your measurements**. In the previous example, the independent variable is the temperature (which you can easily measure with a thermometer) but the dependent variable is the refractive index, **which you can't measure directly**. In fact, the refractive index needs to be **calculated** using the incoming and outgoing angles that you **measure** with your experiment and Snell's law.

To give you an idea of what makes a good research question, here are some examples:

- *"How does the total weight of a bike relate to its stopping distance?"*

- *"How does the drop height of a ball affect the range (as measured from the center of the bucket) to the water splashing out?"*

- *"How does the hanging mass at the end of a cantilever affect the declination?"*

As you can see, they are all simple ideas that try to test the relationship between two quantifiable variables. Nevertheless, if you are feeling lost and do not know where to start, take a look at the resources in Section 5, which contain many ideas that you can use for inspiration.

Once it is clear which variables you are using, and what the relationship you expect them to follow is, you need to carry out an experiment to test whether the relationship between the variables holds or not. It is very important that your experiment shows a **functional relationship** between these two variables, **not a bar chart**. This means that your experiment should produce a function at the end, where in the x-axis you have your independent variable and in your y-axis you show your dependent variable. Keep this in mind when thinking about what variables to choose!

When carrying out your experiment, you need to design a systematic method that allows you to **measure and vary** your independent variable, and allows you to **accurately measure** how your dependent variable changes. **One of the most important things** is to make sure that your experimental method is designed to keep all the controlled variables **constant**. When I say **all the variables**, I mean it. Identifying all the relevant controlled variables is very important since they will be directly related to the source of systematic errors in your experiment and it will improve the accuracy of your experiment.

> **An example:** If you want to measure the relationship between the bounce height of a basketball as a function of the height at which you drop it, one might think that the only controlled variable is the type and weight of the ball you use. But there are many more: The way the ball travels (e.g. vertically), the pressure inside the ball, the way in which you dropped the ball, etc. Your experiment needs to make sure all these variables are consistent.

In conclusion, when choosing a topic, the most important thing is to ask a **clear** research question and to pick the **right variables** which you could **realistically measure** given the equipment you have.

3. BREAKDOWN OF THE GRADING MATRIX

The IA has a total of **24 marks** and five different criteria:
- Personal Engagement (2 marks)
- Exploration (6 marks)
- Analysis (6 marks)
- Evaluation (6 marks)
- Communication (4 marks)

Let us understand what is relevant to achieve full marks on each of the grading criteria.

3.1 Personal Engagement

In order to show personal engagement, you need to 1) explain **why the project is relevant to you** and 2) make sure that throughout your IA, you show that you are **creative** about what to study and how you carry out the experiment, demonstrating **critical thinking** by **questioning and justifying your experimental procedure.**

You can show personal significance, interest and curiosity in the introduction when you explain why you picked that particular research question for your investigation. For example:

"I am a clarinetist and so any scientific study of the sounds that instruments make is significant to me. I was interested in the physics behind musical instruments and decided to combine previous study of standing waves in closed pipes with an investigation into different wavelengths that can be played on the clarinet."

or

"This experiment will investigate how a liquid's surface area to volume ratio affects its rate of cooling. This is relevant in many real world situations, such as how much power swimming pool heaters use, or how long it will take to boil a pan of water – I was inspired to investigate this because I drink lots of tea. It is intuitive that a wider mug of tea will cool more quickly than one with a narrower neck, but I have always wondered just how much the surface area affects how quickly it cools. "

Independent thinking and initiative can be shown in different sections. It could be displayed, for example, in the way you design and carry out your experiment, or by being creative about the suggestions that could improve it. Finally, you can show independent thinking by coming up with the experimental method yourself, instead of following something that your teacher gave you or that you found online. If the different steps of your experiment are well justified, it shows that you have thought about it!

3.2 Exploration

The exploration is about how clear the research question is and how you carry out your experiment in order to get **precise** and **accurate** results. This is an important part of the grade and it is divided in three different aspects:

1.1. Research question.

The title has to be precise (it is clear what the dependent and independent variables you are studying are). This also has to be written clearly in the introduction. For example:

"How does the time that the free end of a cantilever takes to oscillate 15 times depends upon its free length?"

Moreover, you must give the relevant **background**. In the example above, one should talk about moments of inertia, how they relate to the oscillation, and the length of the cantilever. Remember, you don't have to copy your whole Physics textbook, you just need to give **enough information** in order to understand the **context** and **relevance** of the investigation. After writing the background, you should include the **hypothesis** that you expect your variables follow, which should easily be understood.

> **Note:** You might need to conduct research to make sure your hypothesis is meaningful.

1.2. Variables, variables and more variables.

You need to write down your dependent, your independent variables and **a list** of your controlled variables. For the dependent and independent variables, you also need to include the **units[1] in which you measure them** and the **range** you will use:

Independent: Free length of the cantilever (cm).
Dependent: Time taken by the free end of the cantilever to oscillate 10 times (seconds).
Controlled:
- Kind of cantilever used.
- Orientation of the cantilever when it is fixed (Perpendicular in relation to the table).
- Number of oscillations for which the time is recorded (10).
- Amplitude of oscillation of the cantilever (3cm).
- Type of motion sensor used. (Vernier Lab Pro).
- Recording sample interval for the motion sensor and number of samples. (0.1 seconds, 300 samples).

---
[1] If one of your variables has no units, you can label them as Arbitrary Units (A.U.).

- *Point and distance at which the motion sensor is kept in relation to the free end of the cantilever. (Equilibrium point and minimum distance needed for the cantilever to record data).*
- *Way of keeping the end of the cantilever fixed and relative position of different fixed ends. (Same straight line).*
- *The place where the experiment is conducted.*
- *Ambient conditions like wind, atmospheric, pressure, humidity and warmness of the air.*

2.1. Experimental set-up.

You should give a list of **all** the apparatus that you will use to carry out your experiment, including their experimental **limit of reading** when relevant[2]. Also, you should include a **sketch** to show the experimental set-up. It does not have to be something sophisticated, just a simple diagram or a picture where you label the different apparatus. This helps to visualize how the experiment is carried out. If you take the diagram from somewhere, **make sure you cite your source,** but it is better **if you make it yourself.**

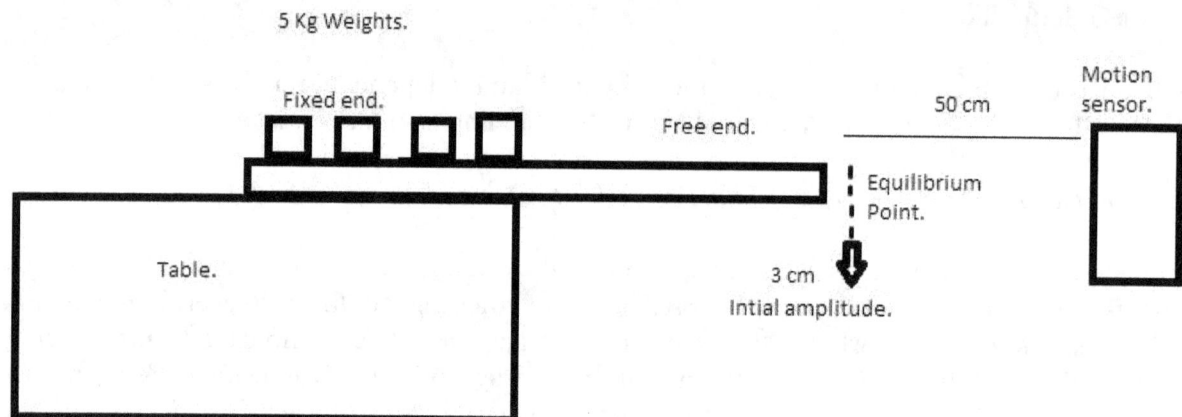

2.2 Experimental method.

In your experimental method section, it is important that you write a **clear list of steps** – almost like a cooking recipe, so that any other student in a similar high-school lab could take your method, repeat the same experiment and get the exact same results as you. **The most important thing** is that your method ensures that you keep your control variables constant:

"*Step 5. Connect the motion sensor to the computer and set the data collection for a number of 300 samples with a recording sample interval of 0.1 seconds.*

Step 6. Use the ruler to measure a distance of 3cm downwards from the free end point of the cantilever in a perpendicular direction in relation to the position of the table, move the final part of the free end of the cantilever that distance with your finger as it is shown in Figure 2 and hold it at that point, being careful to not displace the fixed point from where it is. In this way, the initial amplitude of oscillation of the cantilever is controlled."

---

[2] The limit of reading is the smallest value your apparatus can measure. For a standard ruler this is usually 1 mm. This is important because one usually approximates the uncertainty in the quantity you measure with a particular apparatus as ½ the limit of reading of the apparatus.

See how the number of samples, the recording time interval and the way of setting up the initial amplitude of oscillation **are indicated and kept under control**.

In your method, it also needs to be clear how you are **measuring** and **recording** your dependent and independent variables, and which instruments you are using to measure them:

"Step 7. Start the data collection at the same time you stop holding the free end point of the cantilever.

Step 8. On the computer you will see a graph of displacement versus time. Count 10 oscillations and record the time needed to complete those oscillations in the table below for Trial 1 in sample 1."

Finally, you might need to include a statement about safety, ethical or environmental issues, but **only if they are relevant** to your investigation. If not, just write a sentence saying that there were not significant issues.

3.1 Make sure you make **enough variations** of your independent variable (**5 at least**) within the appropriate range and explain how you are **changing** it in your method. This will allow you to accurately observe the trend that you are trying to test. In order to figure out the appropriate range, you could perform a simple, preliminary experiment to find out what the relevant ranges for the dependent and independent variables should be. If this is not necessary, make sure you include a **justification** of why you are using a particular range.

3.2 **Repetitions.** You need to repeat your experiment **three times** so that you have three different measurements of your dependent variable for each value of your independent variable. **These instructions must be included in the method as well:**

"Step 11. Repeat steps 3-7 three more times keeping the same fixed point in the line drawn in the table using the same cantilever and record the time taken to oscillate 10 times in the table below for Trial 2 and Trial 3.

Step 12. Repeat steps 3-11 setting the fixed end at the different points 2 to 7. Repeat the whole process one time for each new fixed end using the same cantilever and record the time taken by the cantilever to oscillate 15 times in the table below for samples 2 to 7."

> Remember: What you measure is your **raw data** and should therefore be included in a **raw data table**. What you plot during your analysis is your **processed data**, and you need to include a different **processed data table** for it.

3.3 Analysis

The analysis section is about converting your raw data into some **quantitative statement** about your research question. Handling of **errors** and **sample calculations** are key here! As before, this criterion is divided into three sections.

1.1. **Raw data.** Your raw data table must have: A clear **title**, the **measured** variables for all three trials (including the **label** of the variables), the **units** and the **uncertainty** in your measurements[3] to **1 Significant Figure**. Make sure that your recorded data has the same number **of decimal places as your error for each variable!**

For example, in an experiment where laser light is shined through a small slit to study the relationship between the size of the diffraction pattern's maxima and the distance between the slit and the screen where the pattern is recorded, a raw data table would look like:

---

[3] Remember this often depends on the limit of reading of the apparatus that you are using.

Table 1. Raw Data table including the measured size of the maxima (2y) in cm with three repetitions for each sample at different distances between the slit and the screen (D) in cm.

Sample	Slit width (b) / $\cdot 10^2$ cm $\pm$ 0.1 $\cdot 10^2$ cm [4]	Distance (D) / cm $\pm$ 0.1 cm [5]	Size of the maxima (2y) / cm $\pm$ 0.05 cm [6]		
			Trial 1	Trial 2	Trial 3
1	4.7	150.0	1.25	1.30	1.20
2		160.0	1.25	1.35	1.30
3		170.0	1.35	1.30	1.50*
4		180.0	1.40	1.40	1.35
5		190.0	1.40	1.45	1.45
6		200.0	1.50	1.50	1.75*

Note. Values labeled with a star in sample 3 and 6 seem to have a large random error as they differ from the other three values in sample 3 and 6 by more than 10% of the measurement. These values will therefore be ignored in subsequent processing.

Notice how in the example above the errors are given to 1 significant figure and the decimal places for the recorded values match the decimal places of their corresponding uncertainties. **This is very important.** In addition, if you have not already explained the uncertainties in your dependent or independent variables, this is the time to do it (see footnotes in Table 1). Finally, include a note about **any particular data points which behaved strangely** (called outliers) so that later, in your evaluation, you can refer to them and explain them. This shows **critical thinking!**

1.2. Average of trials.

You should add an additional table for the average in your dependent variable. Make sure you include the uncertainty in the average **with one significant figure** and that the number of decimal places in this uncertainty is consistent with the number of decimal places of the averages.

> See in the table below how the uncertainty in the average has one significant figure and two decimal places, so that the averages are given to two decimal places.

---

4. Uncertainty in the slit width is taken to be the limit of reading of the screw gauge used, we are measuring the distance from the value to zero, both points with an uncertainty of LoR / 2, therefore, the total uncertainty is LoR /2 + LoR / 2 = LoR.
5. Uncertainty in the distance between the screen and the slit is taken to be the limit of reading of the rule used, since we are measuring the distance from the value to zero, both points with an uncertainty of LoR / 2, therefore, the total uncertainty is LoR /2 + LoR / 2 = LoR.
6. Uncertainty in the size of the maxima is taken to be the limit of reading of the rule used, since we are measuring the distance from the value to zero, both points with an uncertainty of LoR / 2, therefore, the total uncertainty is LoR /2 + LoR / 2 = LoR.
7. The screw gauge has been checked for zero error, giving a value of +1 · 1 / 100 mm, so the actual reading was 48 but the length of the slit is 47 · 1 / 100 mm.

Table 2. Average size of maxima ($2y_{average}$) and its uncertainty ($\Delta 2y_{average}$) in cm at different distances between the slit and the screen (D) in cm.

Sample	Distance (D) / cm ± 0.1 cm	Average size of maxima ($2y_{average}$) / cm	Uncertainty in $2y_{average}$ ($\Delta 2y_{average}$) / cm
1	150.0	1.24	0.06
2	160.0	1.30	0.06
3	170.0	1.34	0.02
4	180.0	1.38	0.02
5	190.0	1.46	0.06
6	200.0	1.52	0.02

2.1. Sample calculation. You need to write down a **sample calculation of your average and its uncertainty** for one of the data points. The uncertainty in the average is calculated as **(max value − min value) / 2** and should be given to **one significant figure**. You can then say that all the other averages and their corresponding errors where calculated in a similar way:

Sample calculation for Trial No. 3, value with large random error is not considered.

Average size of the maxima (2y), cm = $\frac{1.35+1.30+1.35}{3}$ = 1.33 cm

Uncertainty in size of the maxima ($\Delta 2y$) = $\frac{2Ymax - 2Ymi}{2}$ = $\frac{1.40 - 1.35}{2}$ cm = 0.025 cm = 0.03cm (1 SF)

$2y_{average} \pm \Delta 2y_{average}$ = (1.33 ± 0.03) cm

2.2. Processed data. Before you plot your data, you must decide what you want to plot in order to show the relationship you want to test. This could be for example, a graph of your dependent variable (y) vs independent variable (x), a y vs 1/x or a log y vs log x graph. It depends entirely on the law that you are testing but the important thing is that you should get **a linear relationship between the two variables you plot** (see Section 4.2 for some examples).

Once this is clear, you need to include a **processed data table** with the actual values that you are plotting. If it is a log y vs log x graph, your table will included a column with the values of log x, and another column with the values of log y. Remember to include the errors and do the propagation of errors correctly (see Section 4.3 to remind yourself about the error propagation rules). This table must have the right title, and each column should have the symbol of the variable, units and the absolute or percentage uncertainties to the right number of significant figures.

> **Note:** A common protocol is that the final total percentage uncertainty should be cited to no more than one significant figure if it is greater than or equal to 2% and to no more than two significant figures if it is less that 2%.

If you made any calculations to find the values you entered in the processed data table, make sure you include **a sample calculation for both**, the calculation and the propagation of errors.

3.1. Plotting your data. You now need to plot your data **as a scatter plot with grid lines**. This will essentially be a graph with the values from the first and second column in your processed data table as the x and y variables respectively. Make sure you give a meaningful **title** (y vs x), and **label both axis** with the name, symbol and the units. Finally, you must include the **uncertainty bars** in the x and y values in your graph.

> **Note:** If the uncertainties for one of the variables are too small to be seen, write this as a footnote.

3.2. Line of best fit. Include a **line of best fit,** making sure that the equation of the linear fit includes the **values of the gradient and the y-intercept with the right units.**

3.3. Error in the line of best fit. You should include the lines of maximum and minimum gradient (see figure below) in your graph. Furthermore, include the calculation of the uncertainty in the slope and y-intercept (if relevant for your conclusions): $\Delta m = (m_{max} - m_{min})/2$ and similarly for the y- intercept uncertainty. **Use one significant figure for the uncertainties.**

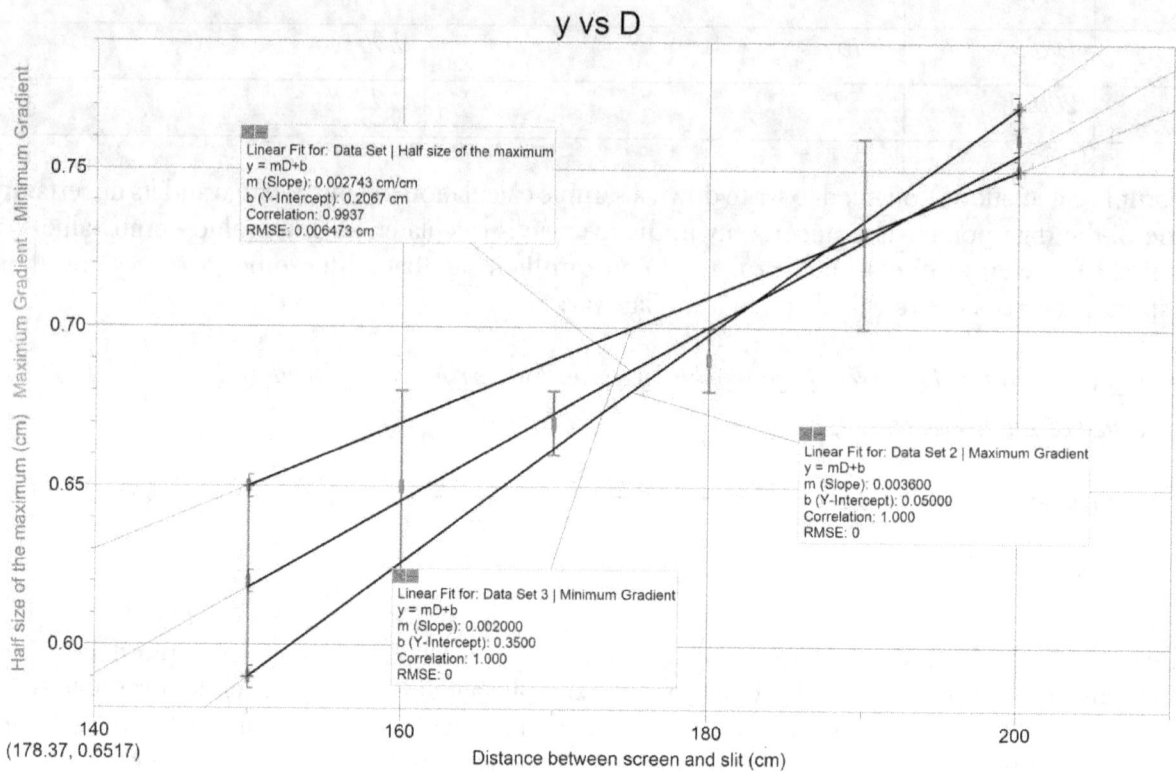

3. 4. Evaluation.

The evaluation is about giving **meaningful conclusions** in light of your experimental results. This is the best place for you to show **critical thinking.** It is also divided in three sections.

1.1. Clear conclusion. Once you have computed the slope and y-intercept and their uncertainties, write down the relationship between your **independent and dependent variable, including the uncertainties** in the slope and y-intercept. Moreover, include a concluding statement about your experiment where you 1) **describe** the **relationship** between your independent and your dependent variable (e.g. linear, quadratic, directly or inversely proportional, none), 2) **state the outcome** of the experiment (whether it supports or not your initial hypothesis) 3) **make a statement** about what your slope means (e.g. the variable y increases/decreases by a factor of m every time x is increased by one).

1.2. Y-intercept. Discuss **the physical meaning of the y-intercept and comment on it** (e.g. does it make sense? Why not?). The y-intercept tells you the value of your dependent variable when your independent is equal to zero. In the example above, the presence of a y-intercept *"seems to suggest that if the slit and the screen are completely next to each other, the length of the maximum will be 0.21 cm, which is physically impossible since the wave will not diffract"*

1.3. Systematic error. If you are testing for a directly proportional relationship, y-intercepts are often an indication of **a systematic error** in your experiment. Make sure you mention this in your conclusion. For example, *"The existence of a y-intercept shows the presence of a large systematic error throughout* *the performance of the experiment"*. Furthermore, indicate whether the **true** value that you are trying to find for the slope **lies within the experimental range**.

> **Remember:** The experimental range is [experimental value − uncertainty, experimental value + uncertainty].

2.1. Sources of errors. You must discuss the main sources of error in your experiment. Here you need to think about everything that went wrong while you were doing your experiment and the things that you found difficult to keep track of. Remember that most errors are related to the difficulty in keeping controlled variables truly constant. Good practice is to divide the errors in **random** and **systematic** (See section 4.4. for explanations of the differences). You must include at least **two sources of errors**. Remember that random errors are related to the uncertainties in your variables (precision) while the systematic errors show an issue with your experimental method (accuracy).

It is important that you not only list your errors, but also **explain and discuss** how they affected your experiment and, in the case of a systematic error, mention whether you are under or over estimating your conclusions with respect to the true value. **Do not mention an error you can't suggest a solution for.** You can see some examples of systematic errors for different experiments below:

- A graph of voltage against current does not form a liner and proportional line. It may be that the load resistance is changing as the current changes, so an ohmic relationship does not hold.

- Measuring the magnetic field alongside a current-carrying wire may confirm the inverse relationship between magnetic field and the distance from the wire, but for the smallest distances and the largest distances, the data does not line up. The induction coil has a finite size, and the center of it is assume to be zero. This may not be the case. At large distances, the radius is similar in magnitude to the length of the wire, and the inverse law for the magnetic field assumed an infinite wire length.

- When using the motion detector, the software was not calibrated with the speed of sound first, and so the measured distances were inaccurate. This error was due to an unexamined assumption, but it was appreciated when the experimental results were evaluated.

- The experiment was done to determine the efficiency of an electric motor. As the investigation was carried out, the battery may have lost power. This would have affected the results.

3.1. Improvements. You must include and discuss **realistic ways to** reduce **each of the errors** you listed. Here you can be as original as you want! You don't have to repeat the experiment so do not worry if it is difficult. Just make sure you explain **how** the error would be reduced and **why**, and that the solutions you give are within technological reach using the apparatus you could find in a standard high school laboratory.

3.5 Communication.

This is common to many IB Internal Assessments. It essentially means that your IA must be well presented and clear. The assessor should only need to read it once to understand what you did. Here are few tricks you can use to achieve a good mark here.

1) **Avoid unnecessary details and jargon.** It does not matter how much you worked on your experiment or how much background reading you did. Include only the **essential** information, tables and results (remember the page limit is 12 pages!). This is particularly important for the **background information part**: Keep it **concise** and **relevant** to your investigation.

2) Highlight the main results (e.g. the conclusion of the experiment), sample calculations, etc.

3) Label tables, graphs and diagrams appropriately.

4) Follow this structure:

- Introduction.
    · Personal motivation
    · Background.
    · Hypothesis and research question.
- Design.
    · Variables.
    · Apparatus.
    · Experimental method.
- Results.
    · Raw data
    · Processed data
    · Plot.
    · Relationship between y and x including uncertainties.
- Conclusion and Evaluation.
    · Conclusion of your experimental.
    · Errors.
    · Improvements.
- Bibliography.
-Appendices.

Remember the last two sections **do not count** for the page limit.

> **In short:** Make sure that the **focus** of the experiment, **the process** and the **outcomes/conclusions** are clear. You could give it to one of your class mates to make sure he/she is able to understand what you did just from reading your report.

4. INTEGRATING WITH YOUR STUDIES AND THE SYLLABUS

Below are some things which will be very useful when writing your IA, although they may have been covered in your Physics class.

4.1. Significant figures and decimal places

We have greatly emphasized the importance of using the correct number of significant figures and decimal places when writing your IA. But what are they?

The number of **decimal places** is, as the name indicates, the quantity of digits you include **after the dot**. In this way, 23 has no decimal places, while 23.00 has two. It does not matter whether the digits are zero or integers, they all count when you want to determine the number of decimal places.

The number of **significant figures** (s.f.) is the number of non-zero integer values which are used to represent a value. The integers only count after the first non-zero integer is presented, i.e. 0.00235 is presented to 3 s.f., as is 2.35. However, if a zero appears **in the decimal digits** after a non-zero number, it counts as a s.f.: 2.350 has 4 s.f. while 23500 has only 3. The more significant figures something has, the more precise it tends to be.

The number of significant figures in a number are an indication of the relevant digits when making a measurement.

> **Note:** The number of significant figures in a number are an indication of the **precision** with which you can make a measurement. The larger the number of significant figures, the better the precision. For example, 3.253 is more precise than 3.2.

4.2. Data analysis techniques.

Your **hypothesis** would probably suggest a particular relationship between your dependent and independent variables. In order to get your data to show a **linear relationship** so that you can compute its line of best fit, you might need to play around with your raw data values. For example, to test for a quadratic relationship between your independent (x) and dependent (y) variables such as $y = 2x^2$, you will need to plot y vs x^2 instead of plotting y vs x, so that your processed data table

x	y
2	8
3	18
4	32

becomes

x^2	y
4	8
9	18
16	32

Here you can find a summary list (by no means complete) of the main relationships you would probably encounter:

<u>Linear relationship.</u>
- **Hypothesis:** $y = ax + b$ where a and b are constants.
- **Values to plot and units:** y vs x. Same units as raw data.
- **Meaning of linear fit ($y = mx + c$):** This is the simplest example since m=a and b=c. The linear relationship is a positive or negative relationship whether $m > 0$ or $m < 0$ respectively. Remember that for the two variables to be **directly proportional** the y intercept (c) must be zero so that $y = mx$.

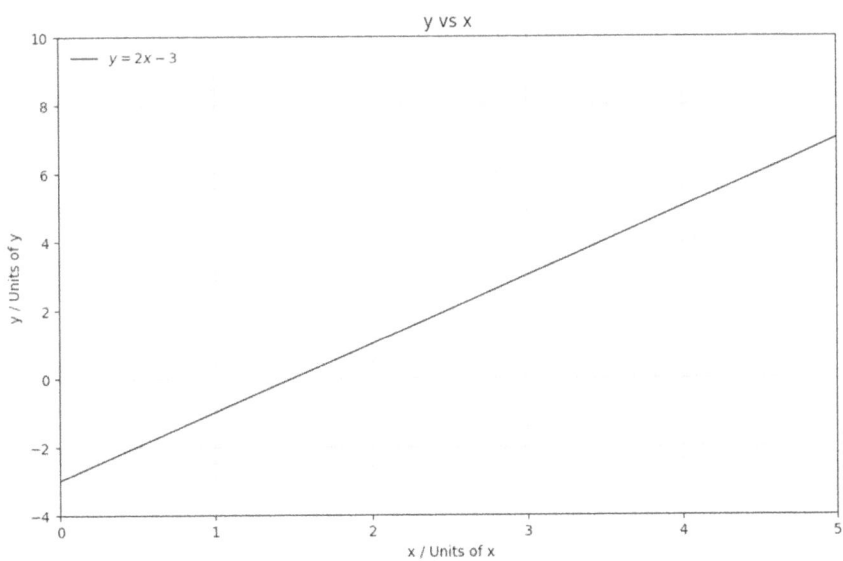

<u>Quadratic relationship.</u>
- **Hypothesis:** $y = ax^2$ where a is a constant.

- **Values to plot and units:** y vs x^2. y keeps the same unit but x^2 has the unit of x squared (e.g. if x is measured in cm, the unit of x^2 is cm^2).
- **Meaning of linear fit (y = mx + c):** Here m=a and c will give you an indication of the systematic error in your experiment.

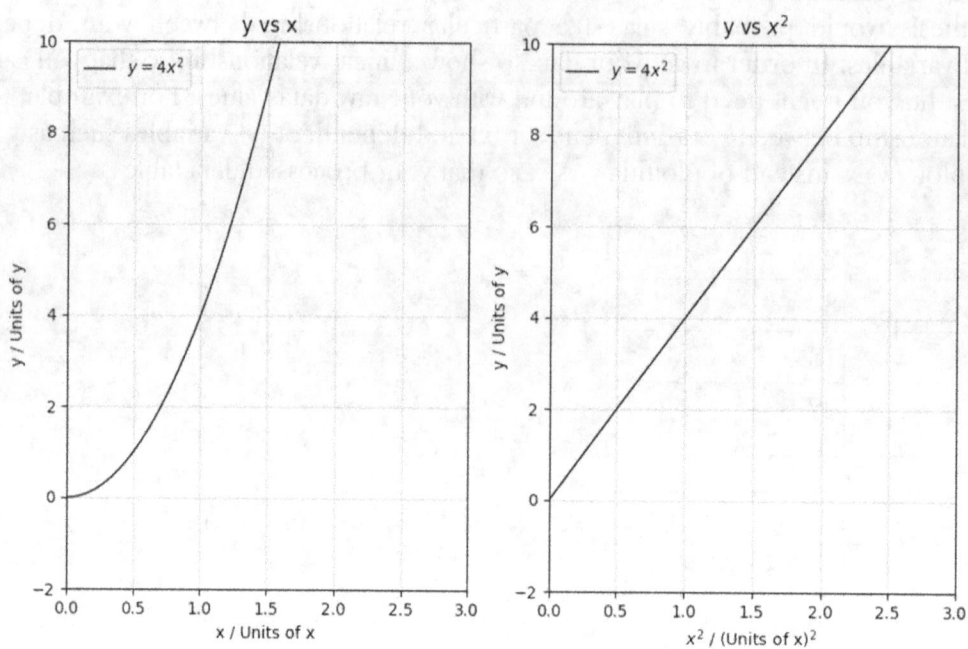

Inversely proportional relationship.
- **Hypothesis:** y = a/x where a is a constant.
- **Values to plot and units:** y vs 1/x. y keeps the same unit but 1/x has 1/ unit of x (e.g. if x is measured in cm, the unit of 1/x is 1/cm=cm^{-1}).
- **Meaning of linear fit (y = mx + c):** As before, m=a and c will give you an indication of the systematic error in your experiment.

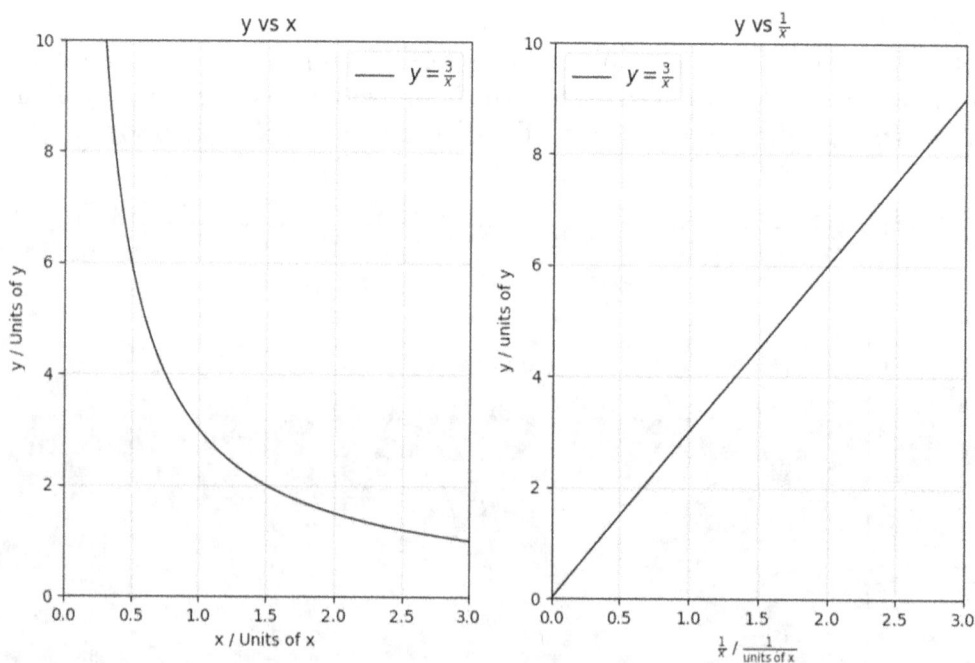

Semi-log relationship.
- **Hypothesis:** y = a log x + b where a and b are constants.
- **Values to plot and units:** y vs log x. y keeps the same unit and x has an arbitrary unit since the log of a unit has no meaning.

- **Meaning of linear fit (y = mx + c):** a = m and b = c.

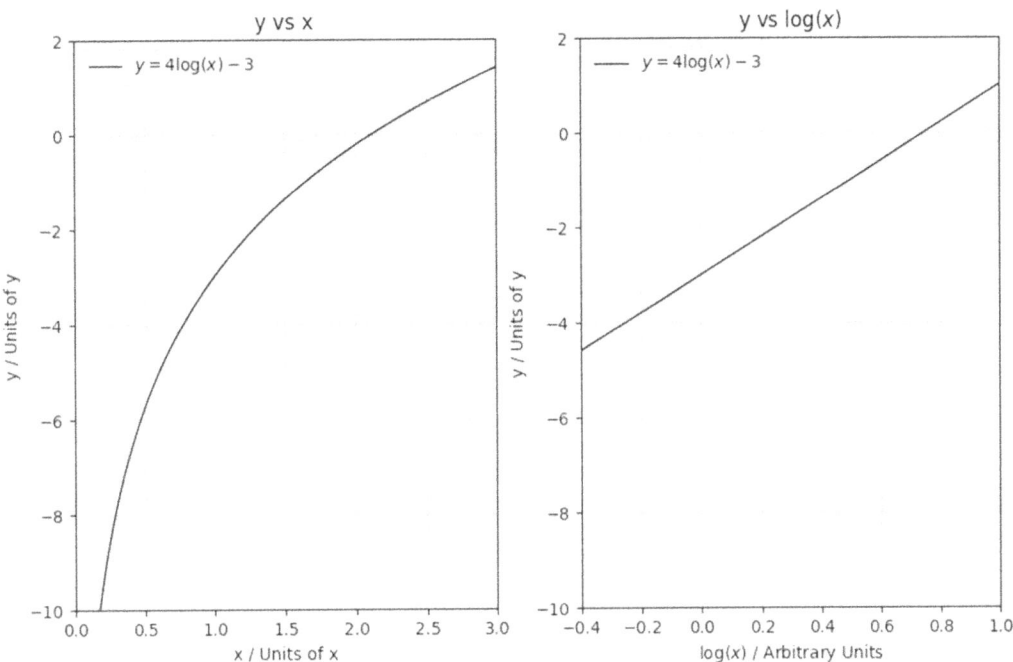

Log-Log relationship.
- **Hypothesis:** $y = ax^b$ where a and b are constants.
- **Values to plot and units:** log y vs log x. Both y and x have arbitrary units.
- **Meaning of linear fit (y = mx + c):** This one requires a bit of algebra and the use of the laws of logs: $\log(AB) = \log(A) + \log(B)$ and $\log(a^n) = n\log(a)$.
  $\log(y) = \log(ax^b)$, $\log(y) = \log(a) + \log(x^b)$, then **log(y) = log(a) + b log(x)**.
Comparing, y = mx + c with log(y) = b log(x) + log(a), one can see that the power to which x is raised (b) is equal to the slope of the linear fit (m) and c = log(a), so that $a = 10^c$.

> **Note:** This method could be used to test a quadratic or an inverse relationship, where one should get m=2 and m=-1 respectively.

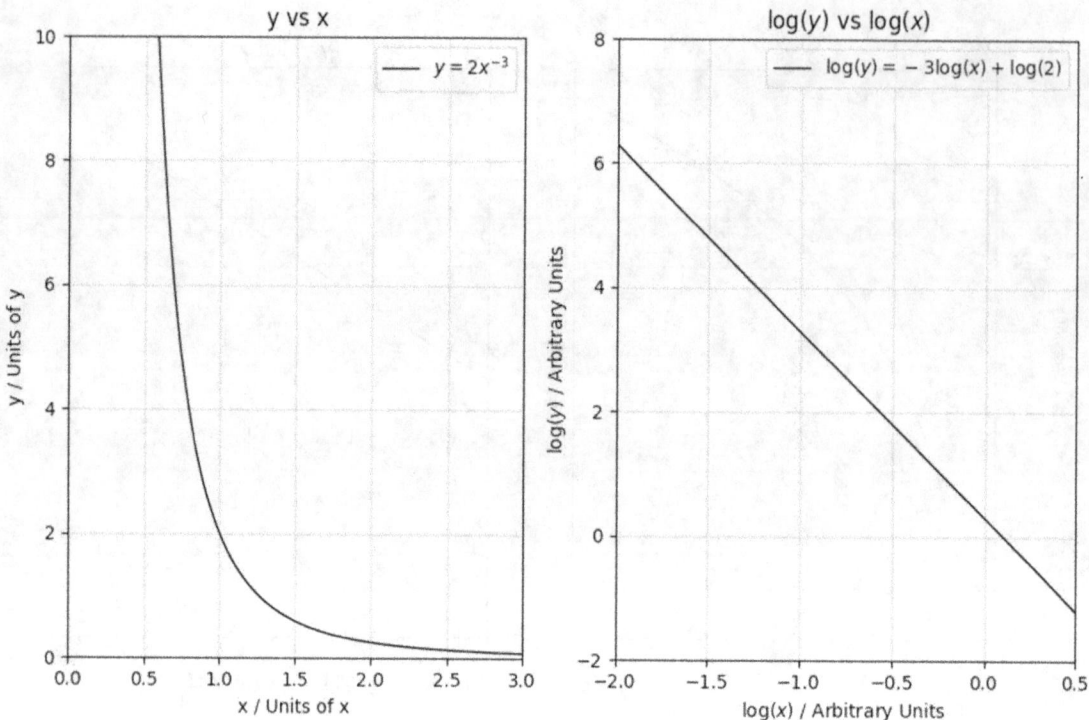

Exponential relationship.
- **Hypothesis:** $y = ae^{bx}$ where a and b are constants.
- **Values to plot and units:** ln y vs x. x keeps the same unit and y has an arbitrary unit.
- **Meaning of linear fit (y = mx + c):** This one requires similar working as before (ln follows the same rules as log), but also, one needs to remember that ln(e) = 1.

$\ln(y) = \ln(ae^{bx})$, $\ln(y) = \ln(a) + \ln(e^{bx})$, $\ln(y) = \ln(a) + bx \ln(e)$, so that **ln(y) = ln(a) + bx**

Comparing it to the equation of the linear fit (as before) one can see that m = b and c = ln a, so that a = e^c.

4.3. Error propagation.

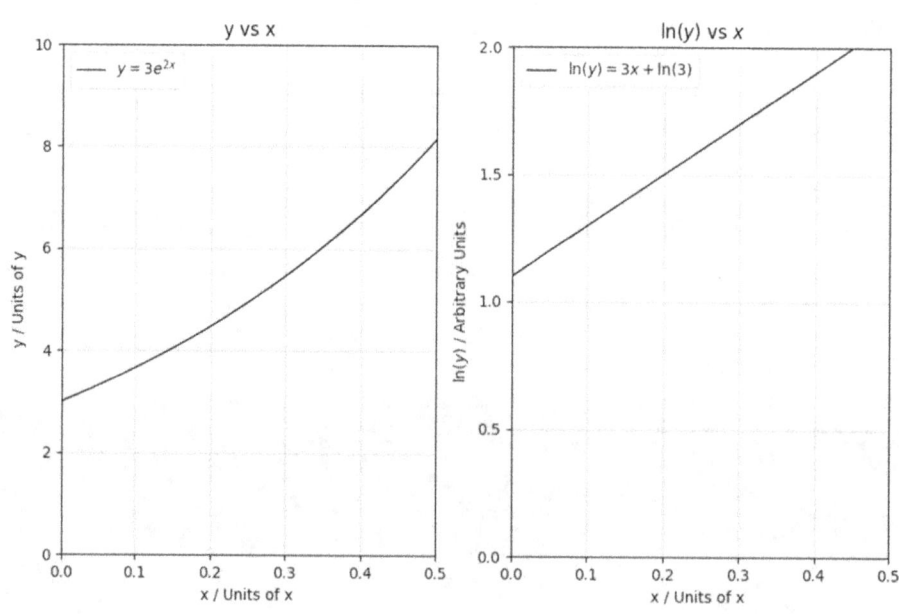

Addition/Subtraction.
For $z = x \pm y \rightarrow \Delta z = \Delta x + \Delta y$.

Multiplication/Division.
For $z = xy$ or $z = x/y \rightarrow \Delta z / z = \Delta x / x + \Delta y / y$ so that $\Delta z = z (\Delta x / x + \Delta y / y)$

Value to power n.
For $z = x^n \rightarrow \Delta z / z = n(\Delta x / x)$ so that $\Delta z = zn(\Delta x / x)$

4.4. Explanation of errors.

Random errors: As the name suggests, these come about due to a one-off `mistake', such as reading a 3 as an 8. A small random error means the experiment is **precise**.

Large random errors are associated to large **uncertainties** in your processed data. These could be due to a large limit of reading in your apparatus or because your experimental method makes it difficult to take your measurement in a precise way. These errors can be eliminated by repeated readings or by improving your experimental method.

> **An example:** If you are counting the number of oscillations of a pendulum in a period of time, it might be difficult to know exactly how many full oscillations it has undergone (perhaps it stopped half way, or three quarters of a full oscillation). This means that you will get very different values for every trial and your average will have large uncertainties.

In the example above, it might be better to measure the time it takes for the pendulum to undergone four oscillations (if it is clear when a full oscillation finishes).

Systematic error: An error due to mis-calibration or an error which repeats itself due to an error in the experimental method. These errors cannot be eliminated by repeated readings and require changing or improving the experimental set-up. A small systematic error means the experiment is **accurate**.

If your conclusion does not agree with the hypothesis (if the hypothesis is right), you probably have large systematic errors in your experiment. These errors might make you get the wrong slope in your linear fit, or it might show up as a y-intercept when you were expecting it to be zero.

In order to identify your systematic errors and improve the accuracy of your experiment: 1) look at the physical phenomena that affect your measurement in a constant way (e.g. zero error or miss-calibration of your apparatus, ambient temperature, friction, etc) 2) consider whether your method includes a wrong instruction, which is repeated for every trial and sample. Next, try to think of a way of avoiding it – for example, using different apparatus, performing the measurement in a different way or improving your experimental method **(be original!)**

5. USEFUL RESOURCES AND LINKS

It is useful to read some marked IB examples:
https://physicsia.weebly.com/1.html

Here are two ~15 min videos going through two **great** IA's:
https://physicsia.weebly.com/2.html
https://physicsia.weebly.com/3.html

For ideas about good IB topics divided by topics:
https://physicsia.weebly.com/4.html
Make sure you check the youtube channels linked at the bottom of the previous website!

https://physicsia.weebly.com/5.html
https://physicsia.weebly.com/6.html

And if you are **very stuck** you can check 300 different ideas for EE's and Physics IA's:
https://physicsia.weebly.com/7.html

6. IA CHECKLIST

You might want to go through this list after you write your IA to check whether you are missing any marks!
https://physicsia.weebly.com/8.html

Useful software:
· LoggerPro https://physicsia.weebly.com/9.html
· Audacity https://physicsia.weebly.com/10.html
· OriginLab https://physicsia.weebly.com/11.html
· CurveExpert https://physicsia.weebly.com/12.html
· Desmos https://physicsia.weebly.com/13.html
· Geogebra https://physicsia.weebly.com/14.html

I you are interested, here are the official IB criteria, guidelines and criteria examples.
https://physicsia.weebly.com/15.html
https://physicsia.weebly.com/16.html
https://physicsia.weebly.com/17.html

Finally, if you want to do a simulation IA:
· Guidelines: https://physicsia.weebly.com/18.html
· Examples: https://physicsia.weebly.com/19.html

Summary of most important things:

→ Clear research question.
→ Variables.
→ Clear and reproducible method.
→ Labels, titles, units.
→ Significant figures and decimal places.
→ Error propagation.
→ Sample of calculations.
→ Clear conclusion.
→ Breakdown of errors.
→ Evaluation of errors.
→ Suggesting improvements.

PART II
SEVEN EXAMPLES OF EXCELLENT INTERNAL ASSESSMENT

The commentaries featured in this section are all recently submitted IAs that scored very highly after being moderated by the IBO. To prevent plagiarism and duplication of results, the appendices have been omitted. The IAs are presented in the exact same way as they were submitted, and without any edits or changes to formatting. We do not retain the copyright of these commentaries, nor is this publication endorsed by the IBO. The Internal Assessments are being re-printed with the permission of the original authors.

1. THE RELATIONSHIP BETWEEN SURFACE AREA AND DRAG

The Relationship Between Surface Area and Drag

Research Question:
What is the relationship between the surface area and the effect of drag on a toy car?

Introduction:
In the future I would like to study aerospace engineering and so far in the IB course the area of physics that I have found both the most interesting and enjoyable has been the topic covering mechanics and motion. This particular aspect of Physics intrigues me as it is not something that the course pursues in detail, however it has a huge effect not just on aircraft, but also on other transportation methods such as cars. Therefore I have decided to work on an example of fluid dynamics, a major aspect of aerospace engineering, and investigate how surface area affects the drag on a toy car. I am interested in how people are able to make vehicles more aerodynamic and therefore decided to discover how the shape of an object affects drag. I have designed an experiment to measure the drag force experienced by a toy car. When thinking about how to measure drag, it is natural to think of a real life example, such as a car moving, and then try to recreate it. However it is difficult to measure the drag force on a moving object. As a result, I decided to adopt a similar approach to a wind tunnel, by controlling the airflow and measuring the force on a stationary toy car.

I did this by using a fan to create an airflow against the car. I used some string to tie the car to a variable mass hanging off the edge of the table, measuring the weight of the masses. I made a small toy car out of K'nex to allow myself to easily attach different sized pieces of cardboard, and with these changes in surface area, measure the consequent changes in force. The basic set-up is shown below:

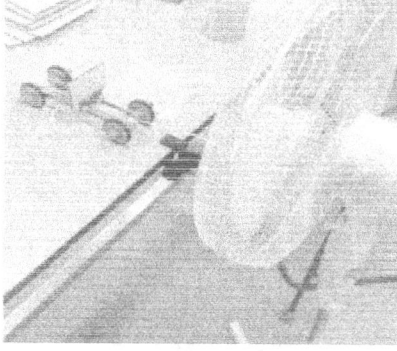

Fig 1.1 – Experimental set-up

Background Information:
The equation that describes the force of drag (F_D) experienced by an object moving relative to the air around it is given by:

$F_D = \frac{1}{2}\rho u^2 C_D A$ [1]

Where F_D is the force of drag on the car
ρ is the density of the fluid (in this case air)
u is the velocity of the air (flow velocity)
C_D is the drag coefficient
A is the surface area of the car perpendicular to the airflow

---

[1] https://www.grc.nasa.gov/www/k-12/airplane/drageq.html

The drag that a moving object experiences is due to a number of factors. Some of these are easy to find such as the density of the medium, the flow velocity and the object's surface area. The drag is also affected by a number of other factors which are a lot more difficult to find, such as the viscosity and compressibility of the air (how easy it is for the object to push the air out of the way and move through it) and the body's 3D shape (known as its form factor). As these are all difficult to find, they are characterised by a single variable, the drag coefficient (C_D). The drag coefficient also helps to simplify the equation by combining in a single term all the different forms of drag the object is exposed to: form drag, skin friction, wave drag and induced drag components. This equation is however only accurate in certain situations. The object must be fully surrounded by the fluid through which it is moving. The fluid and object must have a large enough Reynold's number to produce turbulence behind the object (large Reynold's numbers indicate turbulence behind the object, whereas low numbers indicate laminar flow). In order to have a large Reynold's number, the object must have a blunt form factor (high frontal area and un-streamlined). I conducted this experiment under the assumption that the form factor is dominated by the cardboard, and that the rest of the car has negligible effect on it.

The toy car experiences a drag force from the horizontal airflow created by the fan. To keep the car stationary, an equal force in the opposite direction is required. To do this I used a string attached to the front of the car, draped over the edge of the table with a variable mass attached on the other end, creating an equal force pulling on the car in the opposite direction. The weight of the mass creates tension in the string which exerts a force on the car in the opposite direction of the drag, but of the same magnitude (after varying the mass). This kept the car in equilibrium and, as there is no net force, there is no acceleration.

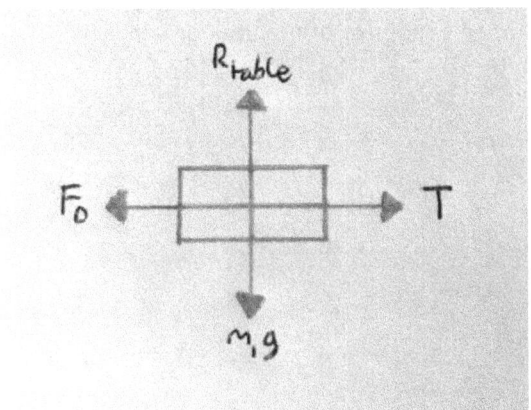

Fig 2.1 – Free body diagram

Fig 2.1 shows the forces acting upon the car when it is in equilibrium where:
m_1 is the mass of the car
g is the gravitational constant
T is the tension in the string due to the weight of the variable mass
R_{table} is the resistive force of the table against the weight of the car (m_1g)
F_D is the force of drag

In equilibrium, the tension in the string due to the weight of the variable mass balances the drag force:
$$w = mg = T = -F_D$$
Where m is the variable mass
w is the weight of the variable mass

Rearranging the drag equation on page 1 gives:

$$\frac{F_D}{A} = \frac{1}{2}\rho u^2 C_D = k$$

Assuming $\frac{1}{2}\rho u^2$ is constant, k is the gradient of the graph produced by plotting the surface area against the drag force. k can be used to find the drag coefficient by rearranging the drag equation and substituting k for F_D/A:

$$\frac{2F_D}{\rho u^2 A} = \frac{2k}{\rho u^2} = C_D$$

By measuring the flow velocity using an anemometer and using the value of density of the air ($\rho=1.195 kgm^{-3}$) [2], the drag coefficient of the toy car can then be found by multiplying the gradient by 2 and dividing the result by the air density and the flow velocity squared. Due to frictional forces that cannot be completely eliminated, as well as the complex frontal surface area of the car that cannot be easily measured, the graph produced will not go through the origin. The y-intercept of the graph will be the static frictional forces plus the added drag force due to the surface area of the car (without any additional surface area).

Variables:

Independent – The surface area of the car presented to the airflow. This was changed by clamping different sized cardboard pieces to car between $40cm^2 - 320cm^2$ with $40cm^2$ intervals

Dependent – The force required to perfectly counteract the drag force on the car. This will be measured by adding sand to small plastic bag tied to car draped over edge of the desk on a pulley; the weight of this bag will then be calculated using W=mg.

---

[2] http://www.kayelaby.npl.co.uk/general_physics/2_1/2_1_1.html

Control Variable	Why Controlled?	How Controlled?
Flow velocity relative to the car	If the particles are moving faster they are hitting the object with more energy, exerting a larger force on the object.	1. Measure the distance between fan and desk and keep it constant, use a piece of tape to ensure car is always at same place on desk 2. Keep doors and windows shut and don't take measurements when someone walks past so as to reduce uneven air flows in the room affecting the results
Length of string draped over pulley	Different lengths will have different masses meaning equalising force on car will change	Use the same string and mark where it hangs loosely off the desk pulley
Measuring equipment used	Different equipment will have different inaccuracies and so will create random errors which will then affect the results	Use the same electric balance
Angle between the cardboard and the air flow	If the angle were to change, the surface area perpendicular to the air flow would change, meaning the drag would have less of an effect	Ensure the cardboard is always directly facing the fan by lining the wheels up with the piece of tape and ensuring the clips on the car are in place correctly to keep it vertical
Change in the humidity of air	More humid air will have a larger density	Keep doors and windows shut to keep the air humidity in the room from fluctuating too much
Friction of wheels on axels and string on desk	Friction will add to the equalising force of the sandbag, meaning there will be a systematic error of reduced masses of the sandbags to equalise the drag force	Add a desk pulley to reduce friction between string and desk but there will still be friction between the wheels and the axels and the wheels and the desk that cannot easily be overcome

Apparatus:
- One piece of cardboard – 0.2m^2
- 30cm Ruler – graduated in mm
- Pen
- Scissors – good quality (to ensure clean cuts and more reliable surface areas)
- Electric Balance – 300g x 0.1g
- "Blu-Tac" – 50g
- Toy Car (K'nex)
- Stand Fan – centre of blades at height of car, (enough power to generate an air flow that travels at least 1.5ms^{-1} so as to get noticeable effects and results)
- Small Plastic ziploc Bag – approx. 80cm^2
- Plastic Beaker of Sand – 200ml
- Small Plastic Funnel
- String – 60cm
- Masking Tape
- Desk Pulley
- Anemometer – 30ms^{-1} x 0.01ms^{-1}

The arrangement of the apparatus is illustrated in the following diagrams

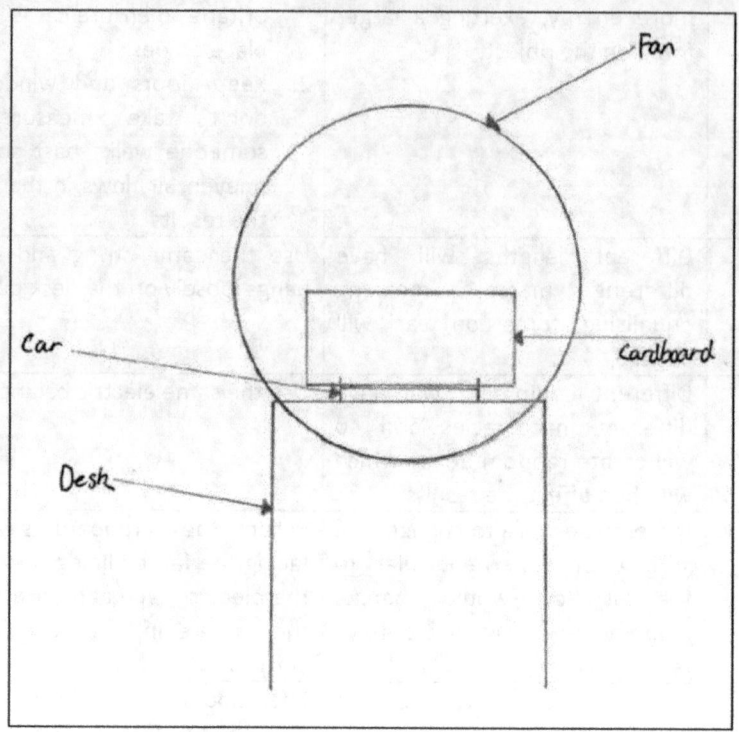

Fig 3.1 – view from rear of car towards fan

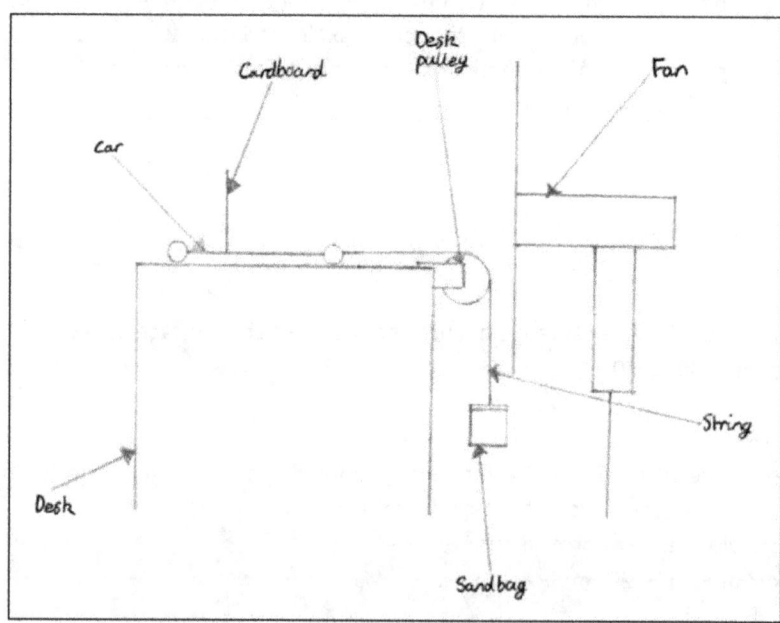

Fig 3.2 – Side view

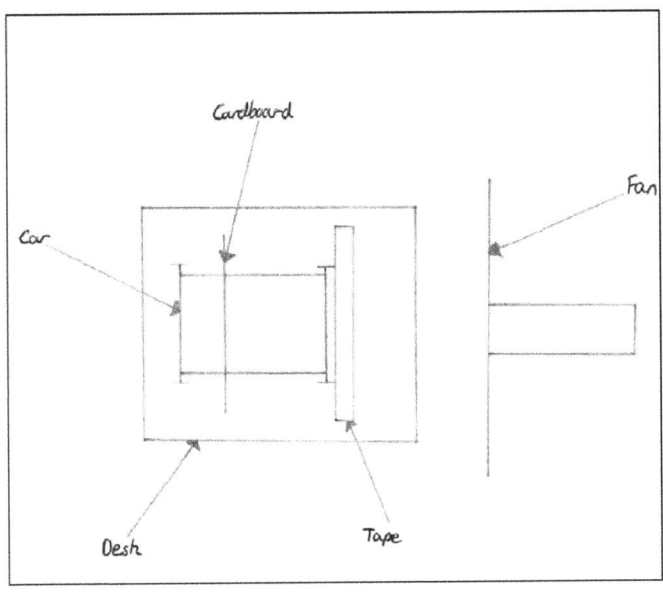

Fig 3.3 – Plan

Figs 3.1, 3.2 & 3.3 are 2-dimensional diagrams showing how the apparatus was set up to correctly equalise the force of drag on the car with the weight of the sandbag. When measuring the airflow velocity, the anemometer was placed at the same distance from the fan as the cardboard along the centreline of the car.

Fig 3.4

Fig 3.4 is a picture showing the 'blu-tac' on the back of the cardboard.

Method:
1. Cut 8 rectangles out of the cardboard (40cm^2 – 320cm^2 with 40cm^2 intervals). When measuring widths and lengths, measure at several points along the edges to get consistent values for the widths and lengths for improved accuracy.
2. Weigh the largest cardboard quadrilateral and use blu-tac to increase the masses of the other quadrilaterals to the same mass. Below is a table for the masses that need to be added for a total value of 19.2g, the mass of my largest rectangle.

Surface Area / cm^2	Mass / g	Mass added / g
40	2.4	16.8
80	4.7	14.5
120	7.2	12.0
160	9.6	9.6
200	12.0	7.2
240	14.1	5.1
280	16.6	2.6
320	19.2	0.0

3. Measure the distance from the centre of the front wheels of the car to the cardboard. Ensure to avoid parallax error by keeping your eye perpendicular to the ruler.
4. Lay some masking tape on the desk parallel to the edge of the desk 5cm from the edge.
5. Stand the fan so the direction of airflow is perpendicular to the edge of the desk and the middle of the blades are 18cm from the edge and 10cm above the desktop.
6. Place the anemometer behind the tape (with the middle of it at the same distance from the edge of the tape as the cardboard is from the wheels), turn the fan on its maximum setting and take 5 readings of the airflow velocity and average them.
7. Remove the anemometer and attach the desk pulley in line with the middle of the fan.
8. Put the toy car on the desk, with the centre of the front wheels directly above the front of the masking tape and the axels parallel to the masking tape, and tie the string to the front of the car, draping it over the pulley.
9. Mark on the string at the point where it is no longer in direct contact with the pulley (at the bottom).
10. Turn the fan on its maximum setting and see if the car moves with no cardboard attached, if it does then tie the small plastic bag (empty) on the end of the string and try again.
11. If the car still moves, add sand to the bag with the beaker of sand and the funnel, until the car remains at rest with the front of the front wheels directly above the front of the masking tape.
12. Weigh the bag and record the results. If the bag was not required then note this down.
13. Attach the smallest surface area cardboard piece (40cm^2) to the car, with the big flat side facing the fan, and compensate for the force of drag by adding sand to the bag until it doesn't move at that position and then weigh the bag of sand and record the results. Make sure the cardboard is perpendicular to the airflow.
14. Exchange the cardboard with the next rectangle and re-measure the drag force (step 13). Do this for each of the other rectangles.
15. Repeat the experiment for another 2 sets of results for every rectangle to get averages to increase accuracy.
16. Cut the string at the marker and weigh the length that was hanging freely.
17. Take an average of the results for each added surface area and add the mass of the string.
18. Multiply the averages by g (9.81ms^{-2}) and divide by 1000 (g to kg) to find the weight of the sandbag and string in each case.
19. Plot a graph of surface area against weight.

Safety/Ethical/Environmental Considerations:
- Turn the sockets off when they are not in use.
- Keep flex out of way so no one trips over it.
- Sand could get in eye, but low chance of this happening so wearing safety goggles could be a bit over the top.
- Be careful not to get items of clothing, jewellery or hair caught in the fan blades.

Results:

Mass of largest cardboard quadrilateral = 19.2g
Air flow velocity readings = 1.67, 1.91, 2.07, 1.93, 1.75, 1.94 ms^{-1}
Average air flow velocity = 1.88 ms^{-1} (uncertainty negligible, see evaluation)
Density of air = 1.195 kgm^{-3}
Mass of string = 0.5g

Added surface area / cm^2	Mass of sandbag$_1$ / g	Mass of sandbag$_2$ / g	Mass of sandbag$_3$ / g	Mass of sandbag$_4$ / g	Mass of sandbag$_{ave}$ / g	Weight of sandbag and string (Drag Force) / N
±2	±1.3					±0.013
0	0.0	0.0	0.9	0.0	0.2	0.007
40	4.9	5.6	3.9	4.0	4.6	0.050
80	6.9	7.4	9.5	7.8	7.9	0.082
120	11.6	10.8	10.9	10.4	10.9	0.112
160	15.2	14.2	13.8	14.5	14.4	0.146
200	17.0	17.3	16.5	17.3	17.0	0.172
240	18.8	18.3	20.2	19.4	19.2	0.193
280	21.6	19.4	21.2	21.5	20.9	0.210
320	23.0	23.3	24.2	24.2	23.7	0.237

Uncertainties:

Surface area – estimated uncertainty based on average accuracy of measuring and cutting out the quadrilaterals

Mass – difference between large and small results for same surface area: 9.5-6.9=2.6g

Weight – calculation with mass uncertainty: (1.3x9.81)/1000=12.8≈13=11%

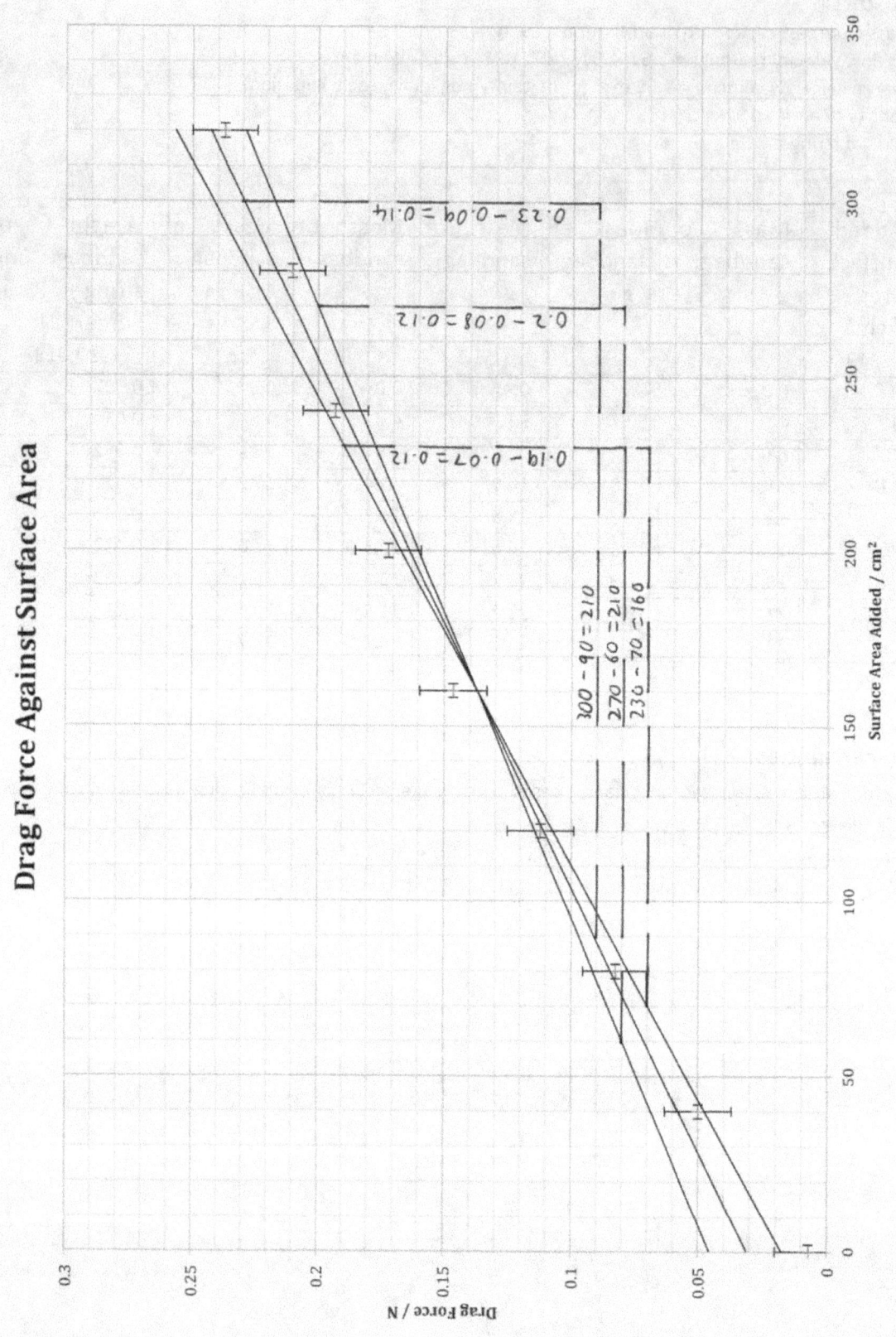

Gradient Calculations:

Average: $m = \frac{\Delta y}{\Delta x} = \frac{0.14}{210} = 0.000667$ Ncm⁻² = 6.67 Nm⁻²

Maximum: $m = \frac{\Delta y}{\Delta x} = \frac{0.12}{160} = 0.000750$ Ncm⁻² = 7.50 Nm⁻²

Minimum: $m = \frac{\Delta y}{\Delta x} = \frac{0.12}{210} = 0.000571$ Ncm⁻² = 5.71 Nm⁻²

Gradient = 6.7 ±0.9 Nm⁻²

$C_D = \frac{2F_D}{A\rho u^2} = \frac{2k}{\rho u^2} = \frac{2 \times 6.7}{1.195 \times 1.88^2} = 3.17264.3 \approx 3.2$

Maximum C_D = 3.55

Minimum C_D = 2.70

Absolute uncertainty = $\frac{max - min}{2} = \frac{3.55 - 2.70}{2} \approx 0.4$

Percentage uncertainty = $\frac{100 \times \text{absolute uncertainty}}{\text{value}} = \frac{100 \times 0.4}{3.2} = 13\%$

Drag coefficient = 3.2 ± 13% (no units)

Intercept by Computer: 0.0316N

Conclusion:

The straight line given by the graphed results shows a directly proportional relationship between the force of the drag on an object and its surface area. This is consistent with the accepted equation $F_D = \frac{1}{2}\rho u^2 C_D A$ which can also be written as $F_D = kA$ or $F_D \propto kA$. This means that if the surface area of an object that is directly facing the direction of airflow is doubled, then the drag force that it will experience will double as well. The y-intercept of the graph was 31.6. Theoretically, the graph should be a straight line through the origin, however due to certain systematic errors that could not be eliminated; the graph instead crosses the y-axis with a positive value. This error is caused by a number of static frictional forces that act upon the car, such as between the axles and the chassis, to resist its movement. Another reason for this positive intercept is that the car itself had a surface area contributing to the amount of drag it felt, and because of its irregular shape its surface area could not easily have been found. This would have also increased the force that was required to keep the car stationary.

The measured drag coefficient of the toy car is 3.2 ± 0.4 (no units). NASA[3] states that the drag coefficient of a flat plate is 1.28. Different experiments would give slightly different values due to different controlled values for the variables. My value of 3.2 is inaccurate by a factor of 2.5. This is outside my calculated uncertainty range which would imply a minimum drag coefficient of 2.7. This would suggest either inaccuracies in my experiment that I didn't foresee or that the equations don't apply fully to my experiment. Some potential sources of inaccuracy could be in measuring and cutting out the cardboard, the uncertainty given by the electric balance and anemometer as well as the static frictional forces acting upon the car.

---

[3] https://www.grc.nasa.gov/www/k-12/airplane/shaped.html

Evaluation:

The main objective of the experiment was successful, as the drag force was found to be directly proportional to the surface area, within the accuracy of the experiment. Although the method correctly gave a straight-line graph, there was a y-intercept indicating some systematic errors. The calculation of the value for the drag coefficient of the toy car was less successful. The calculated value was significantly greater than the published value. This could either be due to a number of systematic and random errors in the experiment or possibly because some of the underlying assumptions in the equation did not apply.

There were two main sources of uncertainty: the measurement of the tension and the measurement of the air flow. The measurement of the tension was affected by the uncertainty in the electric balance measurements and various areas of static friction. The measurement of the air flow was affected by fluctuations in the air flow from the fan and inaccuracy in the anemometer measurements.

The variations in the masses of the sand bags will have been partly due to the uncertainty in the electric balance measurements (3%), which could be solvable by using a more sensitive electric balance.

The causes of static friction would include the connections between the axles and the wheels and between the wheels and the desk, as well as between the pulley and its axle. These would have created a range of force values for which the car will be stationary, with the correct value being directly in the middle. It is indicated by the y-intercept that I may have added slightly too much sand, as if I consistently added the correct amount or even too little, the y-intercept would be zero or at least a lot smaller. To correct this I could use a car with ball bearings in the axles and with polished and oiled metal to reduce the static friction error significantly.

Each set of results had a similar absolute range of masses, which is consistent with the static friction remaining constant, as shown in the table below. This was because the static friction of the car is related to its weight rather than its surface area, and I used 'blu-tac' to equalise the masses of the different pieces of cardboard. This does mean, however, that looking at the absolute range as a percentage of the mean values, the variation was much higher for the smaller values of surface area. Looking at the variation in this way shows that the values for the smallest surface area had the largest variation, with a percentage range of 450%. Therefore, as this implies huge inaccuracy, it was valid to ignore it as anomalous.

Added surface area / cm²	Mass of sandbag₁ / g	Mass of sandbag₂ / g	Mass of sandbag₃ / g	Mass of sandbag₄ / g	Mass of sandbag_ave / g	Max mass of sandbag / g	Min mass of sandbag / g	Absolute Range / g	Percentage Range
±2	±1.3					N/A			
0	0	0	0.9	0	0.2	0.9	0	0.9	450%
40	4.9	5.6	3.9	4	4.6	5.6	3.9	1.7	37%
80	6.9	7.4	9.5	7.8	7.9	9.5	6.9	2.6	33%
120	11.6	10.8	10.9	10.4	10.9	11.6	10.4	1.2	11%
160	15.2	14.2	13.8	14.5	14.4	15.2	13.8	1.4	10%
200	17	17.3	16.5	17.3	17	17.3	16.5	0.8	5%
240	18.8	18.3	20.2	19.4	19.2	20.2	18.3	1.9	10%
280	21.6	19.4	21.2	21.5	20.9	21.6	19.4	2.2	11%
320	23	23.3	24.2	24.2	23.7	24.2	23	1.2	5%

The flow speed of the air also showed to fluctuate a lot, as shown by the variations in the anemometer readings of 0.4 ms⁻1. This uncertainty would have had a very large effect on the final result for the drag coefficient, as it is inversely proportional to the square of the flow velocity. The effect of these variations should, in theory, have caused the mass of the sandbag for which the car remained stationary to vary constantly with the air flow. However the car remained stationary because the sticking friction had a greater effect than the fluctuations in the air flow velocity.

If I were to completely remove the sticking friction it could complicate things, as there is a chance I would not be able to keep the car stationary, due to the variation in drag force from the variation in airflow from the fan. For the removal of the sticking friction to be effective, it would also require other aspects of the experiment to be upgraded, such as a more consistent fan and a simpler way to add and remove sand from the sandbag.

There will also have been additional uncertainties due to temperature and humidity fluctuations in the air as people walked by, drafts passed through the room or people breathed close to the airflow. The fan itself may not have created a constant laminar flow of air towards the car, changing the force on the car slightly. This could be improved by either using a better fan that is more consistent in its flow or even a wind tunnel to keep the system closed. A closed system such as a wind tunnel would also improve the reproducibility of the experiment, allowing for even greater accuracy.

An error in the calculation of the drag coefficient was that the car itself had an impact on the overall form factor. Due to its irregular 3D shape, the presented surface area would have been very difficult to accurately measure, or even to estimate, therefore allowances for this surface area could not easily be made. I attempted by measuring the force required to keep the car alone stationary however the results were too inconsistent and seemingly random, due to the uncertainty from the sticking friction being too large, therefore I ignored them as anomalous. As an improvement I could use a small car with a large, simple surface area on the front that I could just add to, or even the same car but attaching the cardboard in front of it in a way that effectively blocks the irregular frontal area of the car.

2. INVESTIGATING TENSION, FREQUENCY, MASS PER UNIT LENGTH & WAVE VELOCITY OF A STRING USING A SONOMETER

Introduction

I have a passion for music, in all its forms. I play piano, as well as bassoon, saxophone and organ, and I love to perform on stage. As well as a love for music, I also have a deep interest in science, and so am naturally interested in the physics behind music, and the ways in which sound works. I want to broaden my knowledge in the field of acoustics; and in my investigation I hope to be able to do this.

I will be investigating the tension and frequency of a string, using a sonometer. The tension is the independent variable, and the frequency is the dependent variable, as this is what I will be measuring. I will be finding the relationship between these two variables, before going on to look at the mass per unit length, and the wave velocity of the string.

I chose to change tension and look at the effect of this on the frequency of the sound wave in a string. Tension is something that string players fine tune in their strings every time they play – a particular string must be in tune with the other strings on the instrument, as well as being in tune with other instruments, if playing in an ensemble. String players change their instrument's tuning by altering the tension in their strings, which results in a change in frequency (and therefore in pitch). As somebody who frequently plays in orchestras with string players, I am curious to know the physics behind their instruments, and I want to know how a change in tension in a string affects the frequency of the resulting sound. I know that I will be able to measure these two variables – tension and frequency – using the apparatus available to me, and I hope that meaningful sets of data will be obtained. I hope that my investigation into the relationship between tension and frequency will be a starting point for deeper research into the physics behind both the results I obtain, as well as to do with other areas of acoustics, including other properties of sound waves.

Research Question

To find the relationship between the tension and frequency of a string using a sonometer, and to investigate its mass per unit length and wave velocity.

Background Information

The force in any body when it is stretched (or taut) is called tension. A mass on the end of a string means the string will be under tension: at any given point on that string, the tension force will be the same, acting in two equal and opposite directions. Tension, T, is given by $T = mg$ for a mass hanging on a vertical string (as found on a sonometer). The accepted value of g is taken to be 9.81ms^{-2}, as given in the physics data booklet.

Elasticity and a source of energy are the preconditions for periodic motion, and when the elastic object is an extended body, then the periodic motion takes the form of travelling waves.[1] However, when two waves of the same speed and wavelength and equal (or almost equal) amplitudes travelling in opposite directions meet, a standing wave is formed. This wave is the result of the superposition of the two waves travelling in opposite directions. These standing waves arise from the combination of reflection and interference such that the reflected waves interfere constructively with the incident waves. An important part of the condition for this constructive interference for stretched strings is the fact that the waves change phase upon reflection from a fixed end. Under these conditions, the medium appears to vibrate in segments or regions and the fact that these vibrations are made up of traveling waves is not apparent – hence the term 'standing wave'[2]. Standing waves are seen in musical instruments, such as on cello strings – which I will be looking at in my investigation.

When tension in a string is increased, waves cannot move as freely as they can when the tension is less. Increasing the tension decreases the amplitude of oscillation in the standing waves. Conversely, if tension in a string is decreased, the amplitude of oscillation will increase. As tension increases, wave velocity increases (see below); therefore meaning that frequency also increases – in my investigation, I will be finding the relationship between this change.

The velocity of a pulse is determined by the tension in the string, and the mass per unit length of the string. The greater the tension in the medium, the greater the velocity of the wave will be. An increase in tension means that the wave amplitude becomes smaller, meaning wave velocity increases. Provided that the amplitude is not too big (compared with the length of the string), v is independent of the shape of the pulse produced, and how quickly it is produced. This can be demonstrated by creating pulses on a slinky, and changing the tension by having it stretched different amounts.[3]

---

[1] "Traveling Waves." *HyperPhysics*. Web. 13 June 2016. <http://hyperphysics.phy-astr.gsu.edu/hbase/sound/wavplt.html#c2>.

[2] "Standing Waves." *HyperPhysics*. Web. 13 June 2016. <http://hyperphysics.phy-astr.gsu.edu/hbase/waves/standw.html>.

[3] Tsokos, K. A. *Physics for the IB Diploma Fifth Edition*. Cambridge: Cambridge UP, 2008. Print.

The frequency of a travelling wave in a stretched string is given by

$$f = \frac{\sqrt{\frac{T}{\mu}}}{2L}$$

where:

f = frequency/Hz μ = mass per unit length/kg m^{-1} (= m/L)
T = tension/N L = length of string/m

This rearranges to:

$$f = \frac{1}{2L}\sqrt{\frac{T}{\mu}}$$

$$\therefore f^2 = \frac{1}{4L^2\mu}T$$

This is now in the form $y = mx + c$, and so will produce a graph with a straight line, when f^2 is plotted on the y-axis, against T on the x-axis. The gradient of the graph will give $\frac{1}{4L^2\mu}$.

μ can then be found by rearranging the equation and substituting in a value for the length of the string. Once a value for μ has been found, the wave velocity can be found, and is given by:

$$v = \sqrt{\frac{T}{\mu}}$$

Variables

Independent variable:
Tension in the string, measured in Newtons. Changed by placing different hanging masses on the string.

Dependent variable:
Frequency of the sound wave produced, measured in Hertz using Audacity open-source software. Changed by altering the tension.

Controlled variables:
- Type of string (diameter, material, mass per unit length, density) – I will be using the same D cello string throughout, made of a steel core and wound with nickel wire.
- Length of cello string – I will be using the same string throughout, with bridges on the sonometer placed in fixed positions.

- Same 'size' in Audacity – this controls how many samples are used in the frequency analysis; a larger size gives more accurate frequency resolution. I will set the size to 1024 samples for my investigation.

Apparatus

- Sonometer
- Metal bridges
- Sticky tape
- Slotted mass hanger set, 5.0 x 0.1 kg
- Metre rule, 100 x 0.1 cm
- Electric balance, 5.00 x 0.01 kg
- Microphone
- Computer running Audacity software (a free open-source digital audio editor, available to download online)
- Cello string
- Length of nichrome wire, 1m approx, with diameter approx 2mm

Method

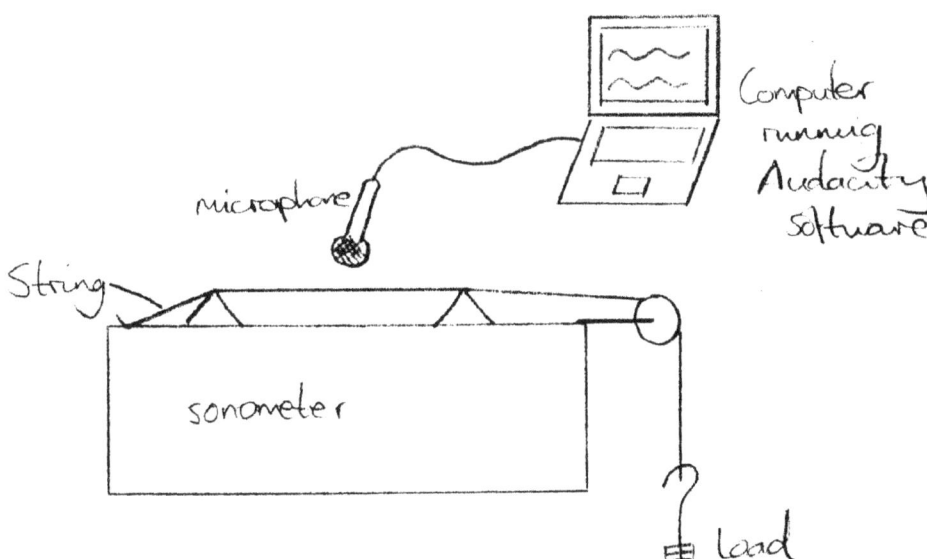

1. Suspend the cello string across the sonometer using two metal bridges. Hold the two bridges in place with sticky tape so that they cannot be moved, keeping the length of the cello string the same. The cello string will probably not be long enough to extend the full

length of the sonometer – if this is the case then attach a length of nichrome wire to the cello string to extend it. Set up the microphone and computer running Audacity software, as in the diagram above. Position apparatus in a room that is as quiet as possible, to reduce background noise, which may make the data that is produced by Audacity more confusing to process. Once a suitable position for the microphone has been found, keep it in that position, so that the distance between the microphone and the string is kept the same. Audacity will then receive the same level from the microphone throughout the experiment, again helping to make data processing less confusing in Audacity.

2. Measure the length of the string (between the two bridges) using the metre rule, and record it. This value will be needed in calculations later on. Finding a suitable position for the two bridges may take some time – the string must be taught between the two bridges at all tensions to be measured. Placing the bridges further apart requires a greater load in order for the string to be taught – this is something I found out whilst carrying out the experiment – however you do not want the string to break!

3. Attach masses to the end of the string via the pulley system on the sonometer. Start with a mass of 1.5kg, as the string should be taught with this load. Record the mass in the table of results. This can be used to find the tension, using $T = mg$. Take g to be equal to 9.81ms^{-2}. This is the accepted value, given in the IB physics data booklet.

4. Create a pulse on the string by plucking it with your finger. To ensure valid results, create the pulse at the same point on the string for each test.

5. Using Audacity, record the sound the pulse produces. Set the project sample rate to a suitable value – for my experiment this was 44,100Hz. Sample rate refers to the number of samples of audio recorded per second. If this is too small, it is possible that not enough data will be recorded to give accurate results.

6. Use the data recorded in Audacity to find the frequency, using the 'Plot Spectrum' feature. When determining the frequency, set the size of the spectrum to 1024 samples, to give suitably accurate results. If the size is any higher than this, the spectrum becomes confused and it is hard to pick out the fundamental frequency.

7. Add a 0.25kg mass to the string, then repeat steps 4 to 6.

8. Repeat this procedure with masses up to 3.5kg, going up in 0.25kg increments, recording the frequency each time.

9. After a complete set of results has been obtained, repeat steps 3 to 8 to get a second set of results. If these results are concordant, then stop there and take an average frequency from both results. If not concordant, then repeat steps 3 to 8 for a third time. Continue as necessary, and find an average when results appear to be concordant.

A photo of the apparatus set up with my experiment in progress is shown below:

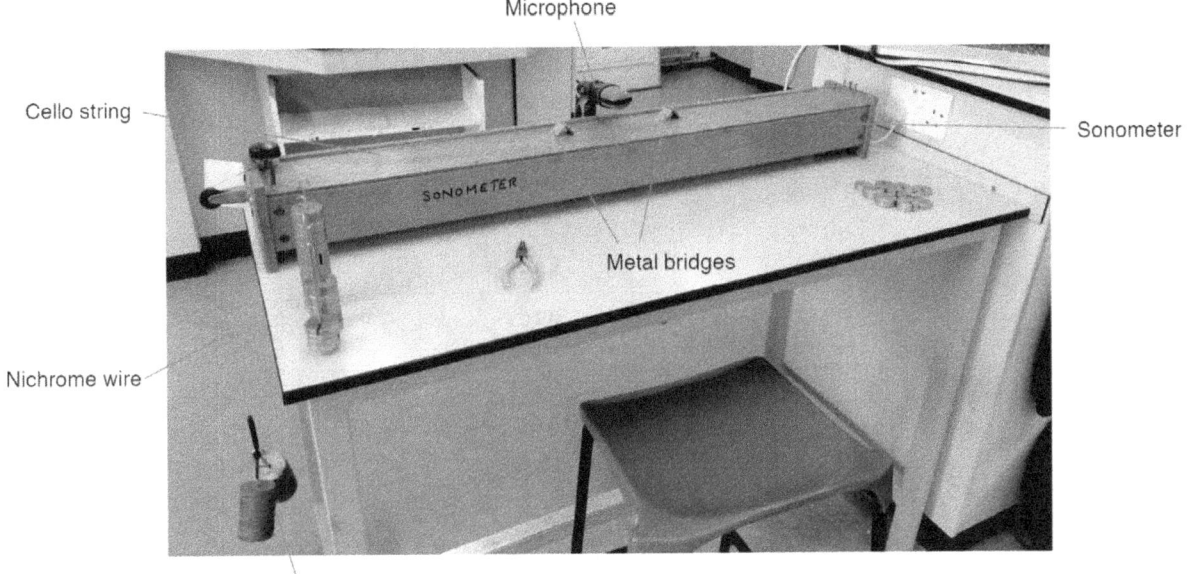

Safety Issues

As the sonometer is built from wood, take care to avoid getting splinters. Take care when adding masses to the string, as it is possible that the string will snap if under too much tension. If this happens, take care so that the string does not flick you in the eye as it snaps. I considered wearing safety goggles to ensure my eyes were safe should this occur; however I decided that the risk was in fact minimal.

Results

m/kg ±0.04	f/Hz ±5					T/N ±0.4	f²/Hz² ±5000
	1	2	3	4	Average		
1.50	194	210	204	199	202	14.7	41000
1.75	214	217	213	202	212	17.2	45000
2.00	215	222	225	219	220	19.6	49000
2.25	227	229	228	229	228	22.1	52000
2.50	235	243	236	231	236	24.5	56000
2.75	246	246	245	243	245	27.0	60000
3.00	250	256	258	250	254	29.4	64000
3.25	261	267	266	253	262	31.9	69000
3.50	268	271	270	271	270	34.3	73000

Length of cello string: 0.21±0.005m

Notes on uncertainties

- Uncertainty of the masses was found by placing them on an electric balance, and making a judgement based on the supposed mass, and the reading on the balance.
- Uncertainty for the frequency was found by using Audacity's 'plot spectrum' tool over slightly different parts of a certain sound wave. I found that this changed the frequency by approximately ±5Hz.
- Uncertainty for the tension column was found by multiplying the absolute uncertainty of the mass by 9.81. This gave $0.04 \times 9.81 \approx 0.4$.
- Uncertainty for the f^2 column was found by looking at the frequency for a mass of 2.50kg, which is 236Hz, then squaring 5Hz above and below this value (i.e. 231^2 and 241^2)

Graph

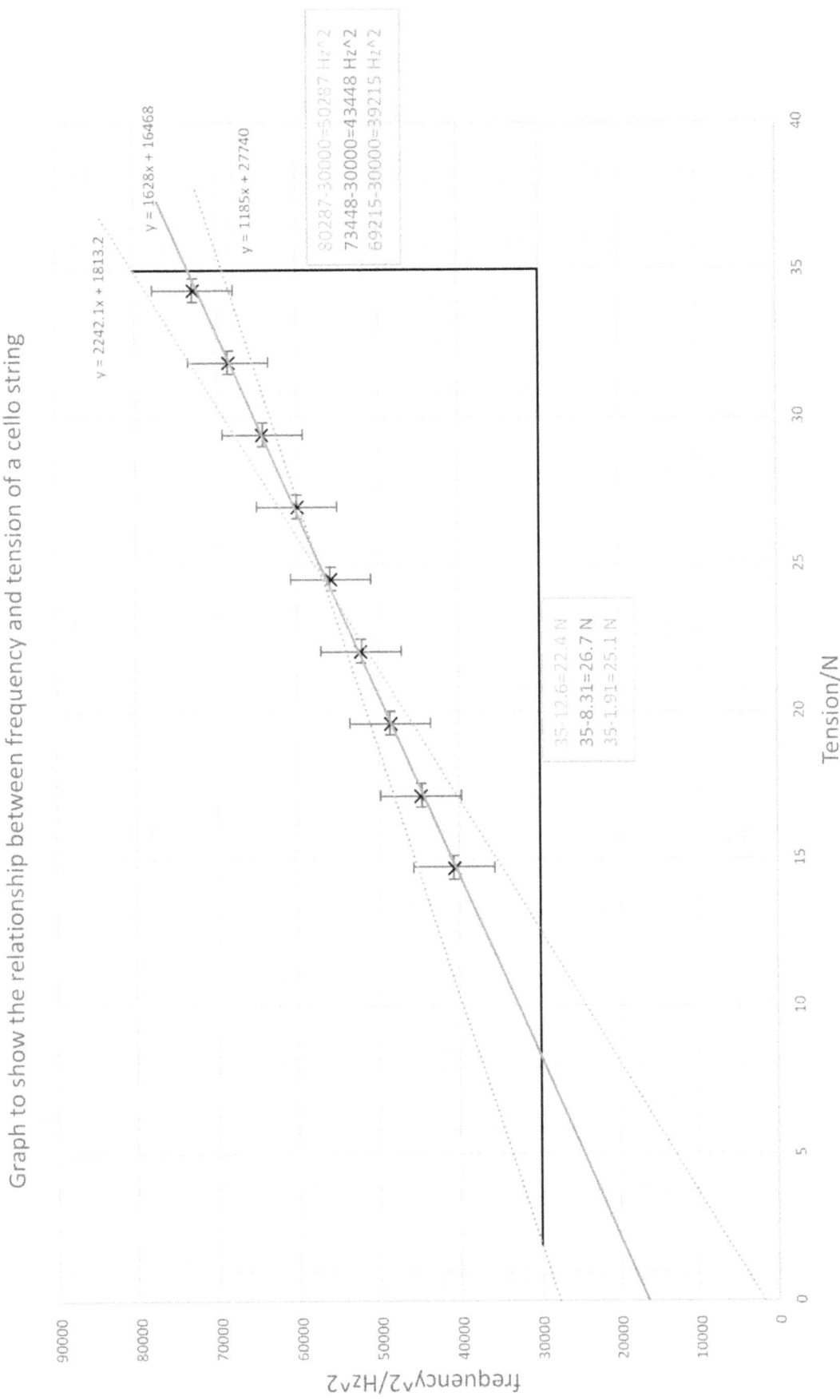

Graph to show the relationship between frequency and tension of a cello string

Analysis

The gradient of the graph was found with the following calculations, using the values obtained from the large triangle drawn on the graph. The gradient is given by $\frac{\Delta y}{\Delta x}$.

Main slope: $\frac{\Delta y}{\Delta x} = \frac{73448-30000}{35-8.31} = 1627 \text{ Hz}^2\text{N}^{-1}$

Maximum slope: $\frac{\Delta y}{\Delta x} = \frac{80287-30000}{35-12.6} = 2245 \text{ Hz}^2\text{N}^{-1}$

Minimum slope: $\frac{\Delta y}{\Delta x} = \frac{69215-30000}{35-1.91} = 1562 \text{ Hz}^2\text{N}^{-1}$

Using these values, I found the gradient of my straight line graph of f^2 against T to be 1600 ±300 Hz²N⁻¹. The uncertainty was found by finding half the difference between the maximum and minimum slopes, to one significant figure. Using the gradient, a value for the mass per unit length of the string can be found. The gradient is equal to $\frac{1}{4L^2\mu}$. The calculation is as follows:

$$\frac{1}{4 \times 0.21^2 \times \mu} = 1600$$

$$\frac{1}{0.1764\mu} = 1600$$

$$282.24\mu = 1$$

$$\mu = 3.5 \pm 0.7 \times 10^{-3} \text{ kg m}^{-1}$$

The uncertainty here was found by substituting the minimum and maximum gradient values into the equation, and finding half the difference between the two results.

This value for the mass per unit length can now be checked with the equation $f = \frac{\sqrt{\frac{T}{\mu}}}{2L}$ by substituting in a value for the mass per unit length, as follows:

$$f = \frac{\sqrt{\frac{24.5}{3.54 \times 10^{-3}}}}{2 \times 0.21}$$

$$f = \frac{83.2}{0.42}$$

$$f = 200 \pm 20 \text{Hz}$$

Uncertainty here was found as above, by substituting in minimum and maximum values for the mass per unit length, and finding half their difference. 200Hz is close enough to the frequency of 236Hz which I measured, to be able to say that this calculation is correct. This is despite the fact that 236Hz is not included within the maximum uncertainty of ±20Hz; however, this is most likely to be accounted for by discrepancies when measuring frequency in Audacity – had I increased the 'size' of the sample, a slightly different value for the frequency might have been obtained.

Now, using the equation $v = \sqrt{\frac{T}{\mu}}$, a value for the wave velocity can be found. When the tension is equal to 24.5N (the median tension), the velocity is found with the following calculation:

$$v = \sqrt{\frac{24.5}{3.54 \times 10^{-3}}}$$

$$v = 83 \pm 9 \text{ ms}^{-1}$$

The uncertainty was again found by substituting in minimum and maximum values for the mass per unit length, and finding half their difference. Although there is nothing to compare this value to, it seems reasonable.

Conclusion

In conclusion, the square of the frequency of a string is directly proportional to its tension, as proved by the straight line graph, in which results are all concordant. The gradient of the graph is 1600 ±300 Hz^2N^{-1}. From the gradient, the mass per unit length of the string was calculated, and is 3.5 ±0.7 x10^{-3} kg m^{-1}. The wave velocity was also calculated using the mass per unit length, and is 83 ±9 ms^{-1}, at a tension of 24.5N. This means that a standing wave on a string of mass per unit length 3.5 ±7 x10^{-3} kg m^{-1} will travel at 83 ±9 ms^{-1}, when under a tension of 24.5 ±0.4N.

Evaluation

Through this investigation I was able to find the relationship between the frequency and tension of a string. When taking repeats of the data, values were generally similar – a range of 16Hz between the four sets of repeats was the largest. Taking these repeats, however, was worthwhile as once they were averaged out, my results gave a straight line graph, with all the points very close to the line of best fit. The horizontal error bars on the graph are small, as tension was easy to measure precisely and accurately; and although the vertical error bars look big, this is because the error on the frequency had to be squared. My answers are all precise, to three significant figures, and are reasonably accurate. Altering the 'size' of the sample in Audacity's frequency analysis may have given different values for the frequency, altering the accuracy – however, I kept the size the same throughout the investigation, making this a potential systematic error. When calculating frequency using the mass per unit length of the string (that had been found using the gradient of the graph), I got an answer that was (using the maximum uncertainty) 16Hz away from the measured value –

this isn't ideal, but at the same time isn't too far off, and may be accounted for by this systematic error.

A strength of my investigation was that tension was able to be measured accurately, as it was calculated using little g – an accepted value – and the hanging mass sets, which I found to be accurate to ±0.04kg.

One thing which reduces the accuracy of my experiment is the fact that the results were taken over a range of masses of 2kg (giving a range of 19.6N for the tension). This is a relatively small range, but it was not possible for a range any greater to have been used – if I went below 1.50kg (the minimum mass added to the cello string), the string was not taught on the sonometer; and if I went above 3.50kg (the maximum mass added), the point where the cello string was attached to the nichrome wire would break. The use of thicker nichrome wire may address this problem. Additionally, I could have recorded more results at more masses within the 1.50-3.50kg range, by going up in smaller increments of mass. Furthermore, to improve precision, a 30cm ruler calibrated in mm could have been used to measure the length between the two bridges on the sonometer, rather than a meter rule calibrated in cm.

Overall however, I believe I carried out a strong investigation, with reliable results produced.

Bibliography

Tsokos, K. A. *Physics for the IB Diploma Fifth Edition*. Cambridge: Cambridge UP, 2008. Print.

"Standing Waves." *HyperPhysics*. Web. Accessed 13 June 2016. <http://hyperphysics.phy-astr.gsu.edu/hbase/waves/standw.html>.

"Traveling Waves." *HyperPhysics*. Web. Accessed 13 June 2016. <http://hyperphysics.phy-astr.gsu.edu/hbase/sound/wavplt.html#c2>.

3. HOW DOES CHANGING THE SURFACE AREA TO VOLUME RATIO AFFECT COOLING RATE?

How does changing the surface area to volume ratio affect cooling rate?

Introduction

This experiment will investigate how a liquid's surface area to volume ratio affects its rate of cooling. This is relevant in many real world situations, such as how much power swimming pool heaters use, to how long it take to boil a pan of water, however I was inspired to investigate this because I drink lots of tea. It is intuitive that a wider mug of tea will cool more quickly than one with a narrower neck, but I have always wondered just how much the surface area affects how quickly it cools.

Newton's Law of cooling is an equation that governs the rate at which temperature cools, and states that[1]:

$$T(t) = T_0 e^{-kt} + T_{ambient}$$

where $T(t)$ is temperature at a given time t, T_0 is the difference between the starting temperature and ambient temperature, $T_{ambient}$ is the temperature of surroundings, and k is a constant that is specific for each situation, taking into account factors such as heat capacity, surface area and mass. Using differentiation it can then be show that:

$$\frac{dT}{dt} = -k(T - T_{ambient})$$

where $\frac{dT}{dt}$ is rate of cooling. From this equation it is clear that the rate of cooling is proportional to the difference between an object's current temperature and the ambient temperature. It follows that for different situations, if in each situation the difference between the current temperature and the ambient temperature are the same, then k is the only factor that changes between different objects cooling. This investigation will therefore compare the k values for different surface area to volume ratios of water. Figure 1[2] shows the exponential decay of temperature over time for water, described by Newton's Law of Cooling.

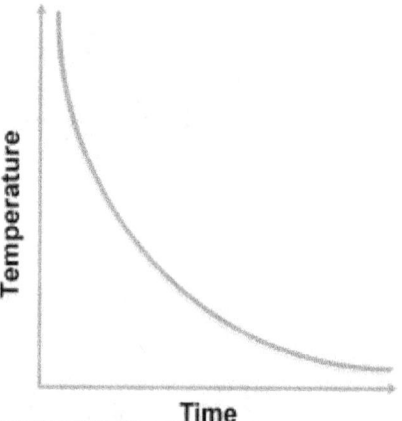

Figure 1 – Relationship between temperature and time for a cooling liquid

Hypothesis

It is expected that as the surface area to volume ratio increases, the k value will also increase (proportional relationship). This is because the water cools by exchanging heat energy at its surface. A greater surface area allows more area for the exchange of heat to take place; therefore it will take place at a greater rate.

---

[1] YAKUBOV, NERIK. "NEWTON'S LAW OF COOLING." THE NATIONAL SCIENCE FOUNDATION, N.D. WEB. 2 OCT. 2016.
[2] "AN EXAMPLE OF DATA LOGGING." BBC BITEZISE, BRITISH BROADCASTING CORPERATION, N.D. WEB. 2 OCT. 2016.

Input variable: Surface area (cm³)
Outcome variable: Constant of cooling (measured via temperature (°C))

Controlled variable	Why it must be controlled	How it will be controlled
Difference in temperature between water and surroundings	A different difference will yield a different cooling rate as the heat exchange as shown in Newton's Law of Cooling.	Water will be heated each time with a kettle, and data will be recorded from 80°C each time. Ambient temperature will be monitored with a thermometer to ensure it is constant.
Position of temperature probe within container	At different points in the container the rate of cooling will change due to different distances from the colder surroundings.	The temperature probe will always be positioned at the centre of the water.
Sunlight/other heat sources	Sunlight or holding the container will inadvertently change ambient temperature.	The experiment will be performed out of sunlight and will not be touched once started
Wind speed	Each of these will affect evaporation rate and this affects the rate of cooling	The experiment will be conducted in same conditions each time with no breeze.

Methodology

Apparatus
- 50 cm³ of water
- 6 plastic containers with dimensions 4x4x4 cm, 4x4x5 cm, 4x4x6 cm…4x4x9 cm
- Temperature probe and connection
- Data recording equipment (computer)
- Kettle

Diagram

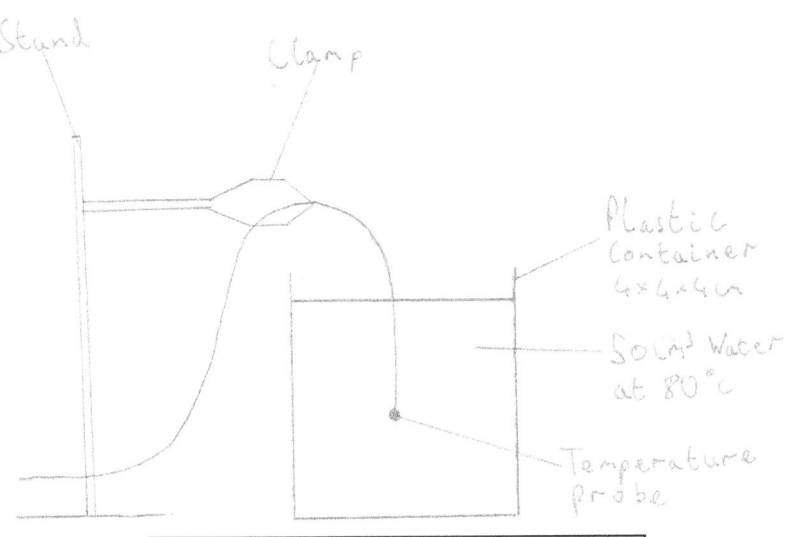

Figure 2 – Experimental setup of apparatus

Method
1. Set up equipment as in figure 2, with water at 80°C
2. Let water cool for 800 seconds, taking recordings at 0.5 second intervals with temperature probe
3. Repeat steps 1-2 with the 4x4x5 cm container, 4x4x6 cm container, up to the 4x4x9 cm container.

Safety: During this experiment hot water will be handled, so care must be taken and if contact is made with skin, run under cold water.

Analysis

During experimentation it proved difficult to start temperature recording at exactly 80°C. Data was instead recorded from higher temperatures, but all data analysis will be performed only on data after 80°C was reached.

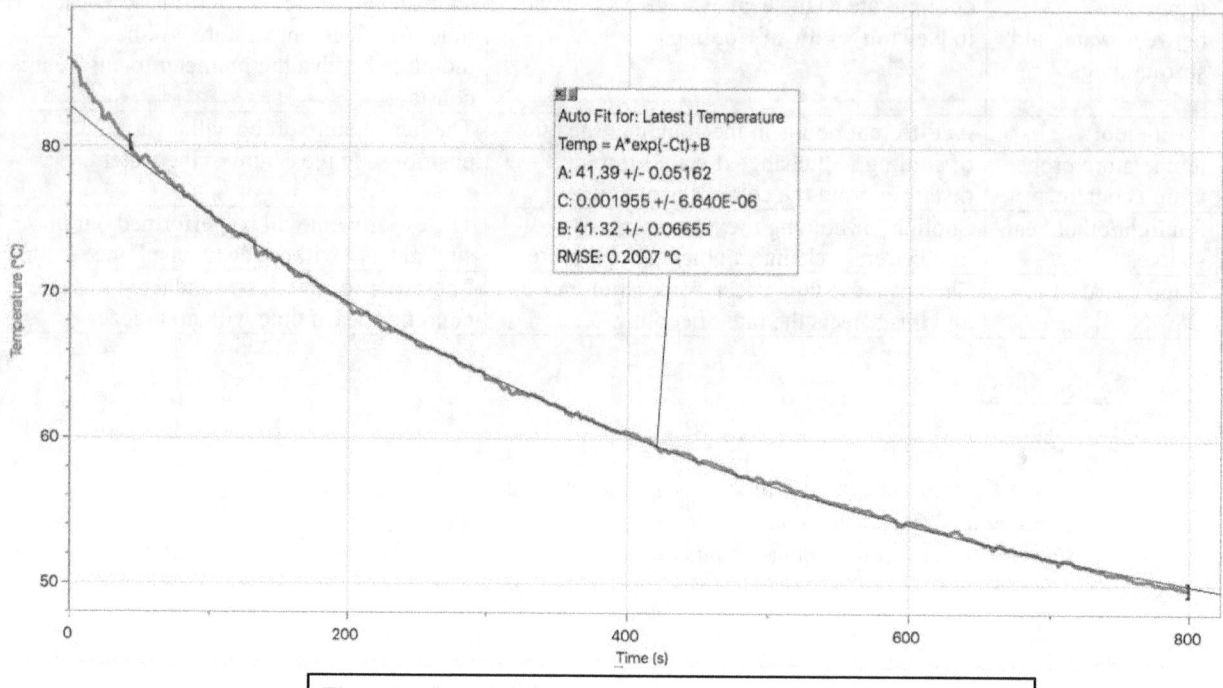

Figure 3 – Recorded data for 4x4x5 cm container with exponential fit

The measurements taken during cooling yielded a graph as shown in figure 3. An exponential fit[3] was performed on the data to yield an equation in the same form as Newton's Law of Cooling. From the B value it is clear that significant systematic errors are present. The B value is equivalent to $T_{ambient}$, but in this analysis of data the exponential fit indicates that the ambient temperature is 41°C, much higher than the 24.5°C recorded. The reason for this is due to conduction of heat to the plastic container and the air above the hot water. As the water cools it transfers heat energy to these surroundings, increasing their temperatures via $Q = mc\Delta T$. This means that whilst cooling the water raises $T_{ambient}$. This leads to a much higher ambient temperature than that recorded by the thermometer suspended in the air adjacent to the plastic container. This explains why the value of B was higher during experimentation than expected.

Raw data analysis

Surface area dimensions D_s / cm $\Delta D_s = \pm 0.01$ cm	Ambient temperature $T_{ambient}$ / °C $\Delta T_{ambient} = \pm 0.05$°C	Cooling constant derived from exponential fit k_c
4.00x4.00	23.90	$1.801*10^{-3}$
4.00x5.00	23.90	$1.955*10^{-3}$
4.00x6.00	23.50	$2.311*10^{-3}$

---

[3] **LOGGER PRO 3.8.7, *VERNIER SOFTWARE & TECHNOLOGY***

4.00x7.00	24.00	2.520*10⁻³
4.00x8.00	24.10	2.775*10⁻³
4.00x9.00	24.20	3.179*10⁻³

The constants of cooling derived from exponential fitting (C in figure 3) are shown in table 1 alongside raw data recorded during experimentation.

The data recorded during experimentation was further processed in order to determine the cooling constant by a different method. The data was converted into a straight line by taking the natural logarithm of the difference between the recorded temperature and the ambient temperature predicted by the exponential fit (B) to yield the equation:

$$\ln(T(t) - B) = \ln(T_0) - kt$$

This new data was then plotted and yielded a graph as shown on figure 4.

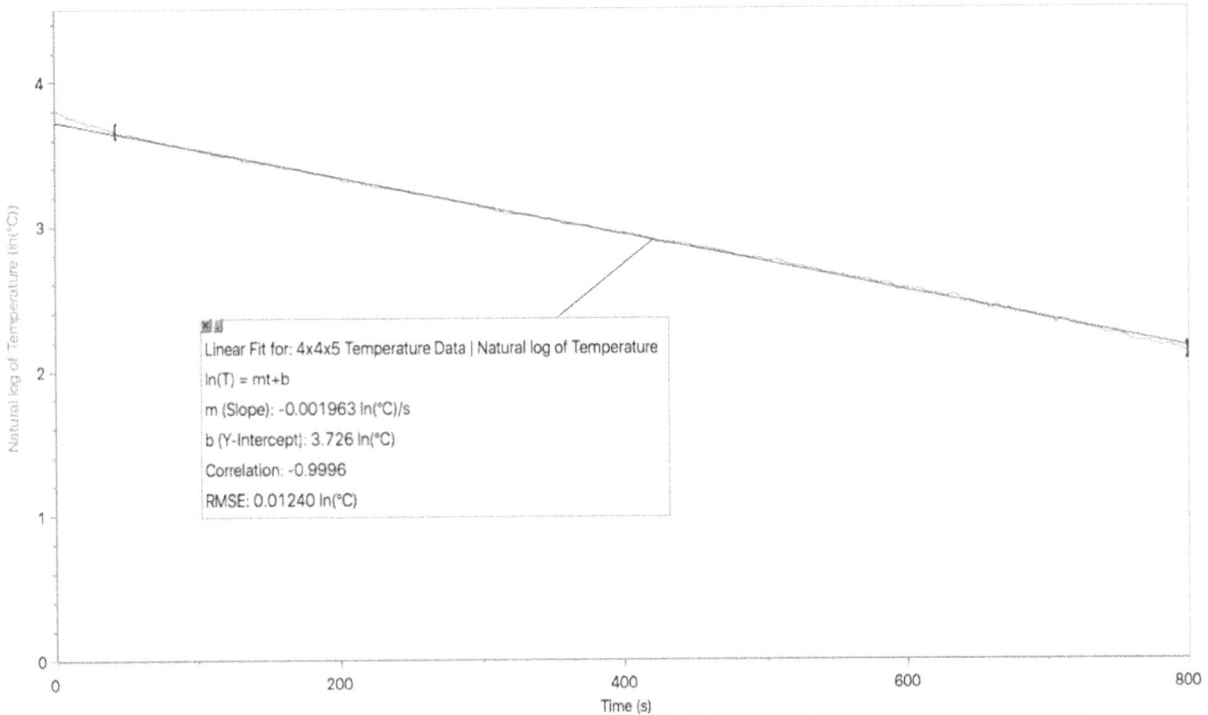

Figure 4 – Natural logarithmic plot of data for 4x4x5 cm container with linear fit

The negative of the gradient from the linear fit yields the cooling coefficient for the particular dimensions, and this linear derivation of the cooling coefficient is compared with the earlier exponential derivation in table 2.

Surface area dimensions D_s / cm $\Delta D_s = \pm 0.01$ cm	Cooling constant derived from exponential fit k_e	Cooling constant derived from linear fit k_l
4.00x4.00	1.801*10⁻³	1.806*10⁻³
4.00x5.00	1.955*10⁻³	1.963*10⁻³
4.00x6.00	2.304*10⁻³	2.323*10⁻³
4.00x7.00	2.520*10⁻³	2.550*10⁻³
4.00x8.00	2.775*10⁻³	2.826*10⁻³
4.00x9.00	3.179*10⁻³	3.272*10⁻³

Table 2 – comparing the cooling constants derived from exponential fit and linear fit

It is clear that the two different methods of processing the raw experimental data yield different values for the cooling constant. A mean average of these two values will therefore be taken, and an uncertainty of plus or minus half the range of the two constant values will be used.

Processed data analysis
The fully processed data is shown in table 3 along with the volume used during the experiment.

Volume of water used V / cm³ ΔV=±0.5 cm³		50.0	
Surface area to volume ratio R / cm⁻¹	Uncertainty in surface area to volume ratios ΔR / cm⁻¹	Average cooling constant k_{avg}	Uncertainty in cooling constant Δk_{avg}
3.20*10⁻¹	0.05*10⁻¹	1.804*10⁻³	0.003*10⁻³
4.00*10⁻¹	0.06*10⁻¹	1.959*10⁻³	0.004*10⁻³
4.80*10⁻¹	0.07*10⁻¹	2.317*10⁻³	0.006*10⁻³
5.60*10⁻¹	0.08*10⁻¹	2.535*10⁻³	0.015*10⁻³
6.40*10⁻¹	0.09*10⁻¹	2.801*10⁻³	0.025*10⁻³
7.20*10⁻¹	0.10*10⁻¹	3.226*10⁻³	0.047*10⁻³

Table 3 –processed data

Sample calculations

$$R = \frac{length * width}{V} = \frac{4.00 * 5.00}{50.0} = 3.20 * 10^{-1} \, cm^2$$

$$\Delta R = \left(\frac{\Delta D_s}{length} + \frac{\Delta D_s}{width} + \frac{\Delta V}{V}\right) * R = \left(\frac{0.01}{4.00} + \frac{0.01}{5.00} + \frac{0.5}{50.0}\right) * 0.320 = 0.06 * 10^{-1} \, cm^2$$

$$k_{avg} = \frac{k_e + k_l}{2} = \frac{1.955 * 10^{-3} + 1.963 * 10^{-3}}{2} = 1.959 * 10^{-3}$$

$$\Delta k_{avg} = \frac{|k_e - k_l|}{2} = \frac{|1.955 * 10^{-3} - 1.963 * 10^{-3}|}{2} = 0.004 * 10^{-3}$$

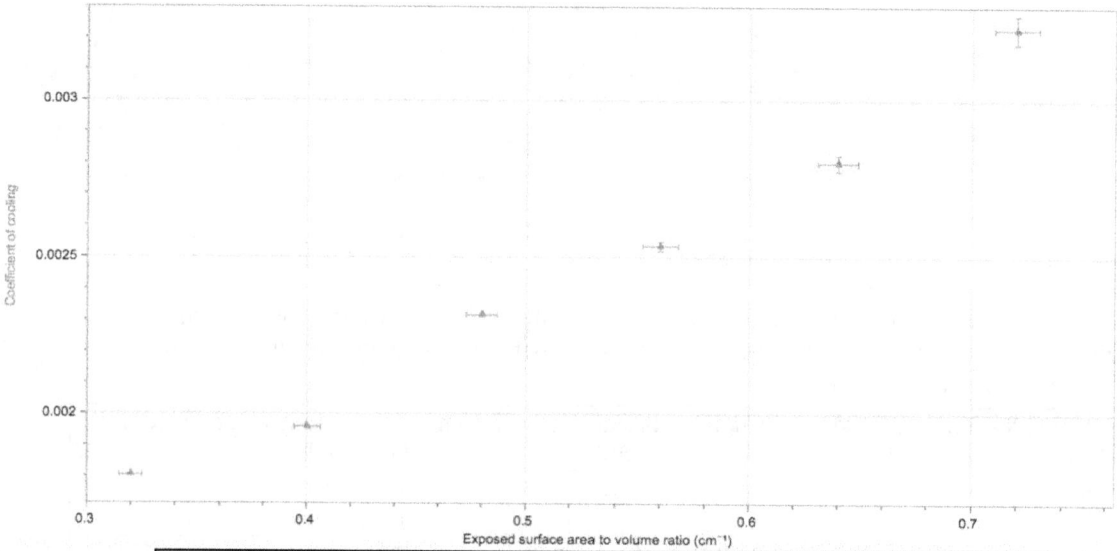

Figure 5 – graph comparing how exposed surface area with coefficient of cooling

Figure 5 shows the processed data, and upon first inspection there appears to be a linear relationship between the surface area and coefficient of cooling. However a comparison of the root mean square error of a linear fit and a quadratic fit shows that in fact the data follows a quadratic relationship better (RMSE of $5.6*10^{-5}$ as opposed to $7.2*10^{-5}$). This is most likely due to the fact that heat was able to escape from the sides of the water through the container and not only the top surface area (the box making roughly a square). Therefore the coefficient of cooling will instead be plotted against total surface area including the sides. This is shown in table 4.

Sample calculations

$$R_{tot} = \frac{length * width * height}{V} = \frac{4.00 * 5.00 * 2.50}{50.0} = 1.70\ cm^2$$

$$height = \frac{Volume}{length * width} = \frac{50.0}{4.00 * 5.00} = 2.50\ cm$$

$$\Delta height = \left(\frac{\Delta D_s}{length} + \frac{\Delta D_s}{width} + \frac{\Delta V}{V}\right) * height = \left(\frac{0.01}{4.00} + \frac{0.01}{5.00} + \frac{0.5}{50.0}\right) * 2.50 = 0.04\ cm$$

$$\Delta R_{tot} = \left(\frac{\Delta D_s}{length} + \frac{\Delta D_s}{width} + \frac{\Delta height}{height} + \frac{\Delta V}{V}\right) * R_{tot} = \left(\frac{0.01}{4.00} + \frac{0.01}{5.00} + \frac{0.04}{2.50} + \frac{0.5}{50.0}\right) * 1.7$$
$$= 0.05\ cm^2$$

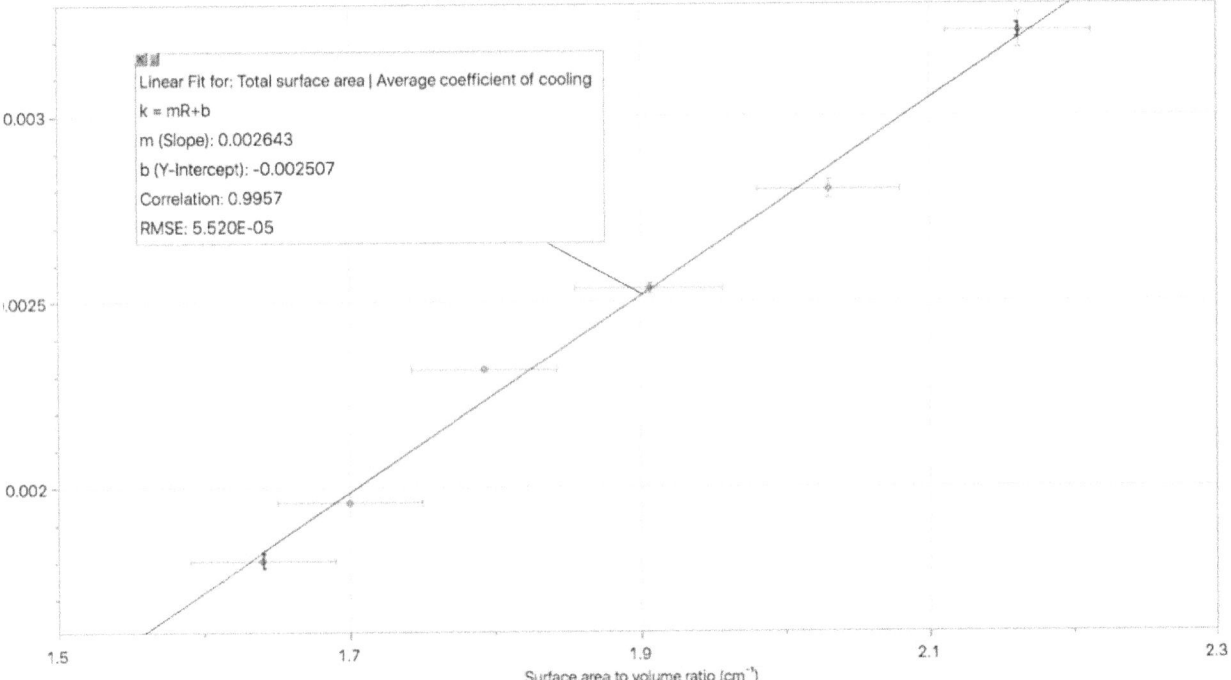

Figure 6 – graph comparing how total surface area to volume ratio with coefficient of cooling

Figure 6 shows the relationship between total surface area and coefficient of cooling. It is clearly a very linear relationship as shown by the high correlation of 0.9957. The point at 1.8 cm^{-1} appears to be slightly inconsistent, and this may be due to the ambient temperature whilst recording that data point. Due to time constraints, the measurement for the 4x4x6 container was performed on a different day to the other measurements. The ambient temperature recorded

Total surface area to volume ratio R_{tot} / cm^{-1}	Uncertainty in area to volume ratio ΔR_{tot} / cm^{-1}	Average cooling constant k_{avg}	Uncertainty in cooling constant Δk_{avg}
1.64	0.05	$1.804*10^{-3}$	$0.003*10^{-3}$
1.70	0.05	$1.959*10^{-3}$	$0.004*10^{-3}$
1.89	0.05	$2.317*10^{-3}$	$0.006*10^{-3}$
1.91	0.05	$2.535*10^{-3}$	$0.015*10^{-3}$
2.03	0.05	$2.801*10^{-3}$	$0.025*10^{-3}$
2.26	0.05	$3.226*10^{-3}$	$0.047*10^{-3}$

Table 4 – processed data with total surface area

during data collection was 0.4°C lower than at any other point, and this may have lead to a higher cooling rate (and hence higher coefficient of cooling) than would be expected.

Excluding the point at 1.8 cm^{-1}, the correlation becomes 0.9989, and the relationship between coefficient of cooling and total exposed surface area predicted by the experiment is $k = 0.00269R_{tot} - 0.00260$. Including minimum and maximum gradients and y-intercepts this relationship becomes:

$$k = (2.69 \pm 0.60) * 10^{-3} R_{tot} - (2.60 \pm 1.11) * 10^{-3}$$

It is again clear from this equation that significant systematic errors are present. One would expect the y-intercept to be 0. This is because, for a theoretical container with no surface area, or an infinitely large volume, there should be no cooling (as there will either be no surface to exchange heat on, or the volume will be so large that any heat loss will have a negligible effect on the water's total temperature). The reason for this systematic uncertainty is again the insulation provided by the walls of the container and the air that is heated above the water's top surface. This insulation means all the measurements have rates of cooling that are lower than if the liquid was allowed to exchange heat on all surfaces freely. If heat was allowed to exchange freely the greater rates of cooling would mean all data points would shift upwards, and the

Weakness	Type of error/ it's effect	Improvement
Insulation provided by walls of container and air above hot water.	Systematic. The most significant source of error. Insulation meant heat was exchanged more slowly and the cooling constant was therefore lower.	Use very thin walls made of a material with high thermal conductivity (copper). Have a fan blowing over the surface of the water to prevent hot air accumulating above top surface (effect of evaporation would need to be taken into account).
Inaccuracy in volume measurement	Random. The 1% uncertainty in volume increased the uncertainty in R by 2% (due to it also being used to calculate the height of the water).	Using a mass balance with 2 decimal places to find volume using density (taking temperature into account).
Inaccuracy in measurements of container dimensions.	Random. On average this uncertainty increased the uncertainty in R by 1%.	Use more precise calipers (which have an uncertainty of ±0.005 cm).
Ambient room temperature could not be kept constant.	Random, although could be predicted. A higher ambient room temperature led to a lower constant of cooling due to a lower difference in temperatures and vice versa.	Perform all the experiments simultaneously next to one another.

relationship relating the surface area to volume ratio and the constant of cooling would go through the origin.

Conclusion

During this experiment it was empirically calculated that the relationship between total surface area to volume ratio and the constant of cooling for the experimental setup is $k = (2.69 \pm 0.60) * 10^{-3} R - (2.60 \pm 1.11) * 10^{-3}$. The very high correlation of 0.9989 makes this a reliable result, however the systematic uncertainty discussed means this relationship holds only for this specific experimental setup.

In order to further extend this investigation water could be cooled in containers of differing wall thicknesses. The results from this could then be extrapolated to a container with a theoretical wall thickness of 0 in order to find the accurate relationship between R and k.

Evaluation

Newton's Law of Cooling applies when there is only conduction, whereas in most situations there is also radiation and convection[4]. This means that the cooling rate predicted by Newton's Law should actually not have been followed when this experiment was carried out, as heat losses from radiation would have increased the cooling rate by a different factor than simply the difference between the object's temperature and the ambient temperature. In order to account for these methods of heat transfer, the experiment could be carried out with forced convection, and reflective insulation to reduce heat radiation. This would have allowed the experiment to more accurately reflect the cooling described by Newton's Law.

---

[4] HARRIS, STEVEN B. "WHAT'S WRONG WITH NEWTON'S LAW OF COOLING." *QUORA*. SCHOOL OF MEDICINE UCLA, 30 JUNE 2015. WEB. 7 NOV. 2016.

4. THE RELATIONSHIP BETWEEN TEMPERATURE AND COEFFICIENT OF RESTITUTION

Relationship between temperature and coefficient of restitution

Research Question:

How does the temperature of a ball affect its coefficient of restitution when dropped from a fixed height of 1m?

Variables:

Input: Temperature of Ball
Output: Coefficient of Restitution

Background information:

During this experiment, the output or dependent variable will be the coefficient of restitution. The coefficient of restitution is a method through which the elasticity or restitution of a collision can be mathematically demonstrated. For the collisions of two moving objects, it is defined as the ratio of the difference in the bounce velocities and the difference in the approach velocities.[1]

$$C_r = \frac{u_a - u_b}{v_a - v_b}$$

u_a = bounce velocity of object a
u_b = bounce velcoty of object b
v_a = approach velocity of object a
v_b = approach velocity of object b

If the collision is perfectly elastic, the coefficient of restitution will be 1. For real-world, inelastic collisions, the coefficient will be between 0 and 1. As this experiment deals with the collisions of a moving object, the ball, with a stationary object, the ground, a simplified version of this equation can be used:

$C_r = \dfrac{u}{v}$	u = ball's bounce velocity $\quad$ v = ball's approach velocity
$C_r = \dfrac{\sqrt{2gh}}{\sqrt{2gH}}$	If the ball is dropped from rest and, when it comes into contact with the ground, comes to rest for a fraction of a second, the equation of motion $v = \sqrt{u^2 + 2gh}$ can be applied but as the initial velocity is 0, it is quite simply: $v = \sqrt{2gh}$ $\quad$ h = ball's bounce height $\quad$ H = ball's drop height
$C_r = \dfrac{\sqrt{h}}{\sqrt{H}}$	After simplifying this the final equation includes only the height of drop and height of bounce.

The input variable or dependent variable will be the temperature of the ball. As we are dealing with a ball filled with a gas, air, we can discuss it in terms of the ideal gas law:

$$Pressure \times Volume = Number\ of\ moles \times Gas\ Constant \times Temperature$$

---

[1] Adli Haron and K. A. Ismail. "Coefficient of Restitution of Sports Balls: A Normal Drop Test." *IOP Conference Series: Materials Science and Engineering* 36.1 (2012): n. pag. Web. 7 May 2016

In this experiment, we assume that the volume will stay constant while the temperature changes. For this to happen the pressure must change too and in this case the pressure is proportional to the temperature. The change taking place between trials (as the ball's temperature changes) is isochoric – work being done on the system causes the pressure and temperature to change but the volume remains constant. The kinetic energy being transferred to the ball through the temperature it changes it is exposed to is equal to the work done.

It is clear that the lower the pressure inside the ball the easier it is to deform the ball during the bounce as pressure is the force exerted per unit area. It is this outwards force which allows the ball to hold its shape and thus resist deformation. If the ball is easier to deform, the bounce will take a longer amount of time. When considering the momentum of the ball during collision, and noting that: $F = \frac{\Delta p}{t}$ and if the change in momentum is equal for every bounce, as the drop velocity and mass will be the same, the force is inversely proportional to the time of contact. Therefore, a greater force will be exerted by the ball onto the ground when the time of contact is shorter. Applying Newton's Third law, the amount of force exerted by the ball onto the ground is equal to that of the force exerted by the floor on the ball.

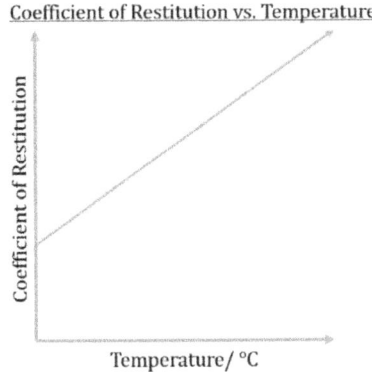

Figure 1: Predicted Relationship

Therefore, the force exerted by the floor is inversely proportional to the time of contact and as the contact time is inversely proportional to the pressure of the ball, the pressure of the ball is proportional to the force exerted by the ground upon impact. Overall, the force supplied by the ground is proportional to the bounce height and so it can be inferred that the higher the temperature, the higher the coefficient of restitution. The predicted relationship is noted in figure 1, it does not go through the origin as this would represent a coefficient of restitution of 0, which is impossible as that would mean no energy remains after the collision whatsoever.

Control Variables:

	Why it has to be controlled?	How it is going to be controlled?
Ball's initial air pressure	As the temperature is changed, the pressure of the ball will change but the pressure of the ball at room temperature will have to be constant for every trial. If initial pressure is higher for a particular trial, the results will be skewed towards a higher coefficient of restitution.	Before placing the ball in the bath of water to change its temperature, the pressure will be noted and adjusted.
Ball's volume	In the ideal gas law, for the temperature to be proportional to the pressure, the volume must not change. Between trials, if the volume has changed, the temperature will have a disproportionate effect on the pressure and that will affect the rebound height.	The same ball will be used during each trial with a fixed diameter.
Bounce Surface Elasticity	The transfer of energy during the collisions depends on the elasticity of surface that the ball is bouncing upon. Using difference surfaces will cause different	Each trial will be undertaken on the same tiled flooring.

	elasticities and therefore will skew the bounce height and the coefficient of restitution	
Elasticity of the ball's material	Similarly, as with the bounce surface, the energy transfer depends on the material with which the ball is made. If the material is more elastic, it will allow for compression and retain more energy. As the balls, will be placed in water, there is the problem of them being wet which will affect the bounce height and yield lower values for the coefficient of restitution.	The same ball, will be used for each trial and it will be dried when taken out of the water with a dry towel.
Bounce height	The coefficient of restitution depends on the drop velocity of the ball. As this is defined by the square root of twice the height drop times the gravitational field strength, therefore ensuring the height dropped is the same will ensure the velocity is the same too.	The ball will be dropped from 1 m each time.

Method:

1. Pump the football with an air pump until a pressure of 135kpa is achieved, use a pressure sensor to check for this value.
2. Record the room temperature.
3. Place meter rule vertically using clamps stand to hold it up.
4. Place a camera 1.5m from the ruler and 0.5 m above the ground as to reduce parallax error.
5. Hold ball so that the bottom of the ball is at the 1 m mark.
6. Start recording with the camera.
7. Drop the ball and allow it to bounce at least once.
8. Place ball in baths of water at 30°C, 40°C, 50°C, 60°C, 70°C, 80°C and repeat steps 1-6.
9. Record the pressure of the ball after it has been removed from the water with a pressure sensor.
10. Record the temperature of the balls after it has been removed from the water with an infrared temperature sensor.
11. Quickly wipe the ball with a dry towel and then drop it from 1 m.
12. Repeat steps 8-10 3 times for each temperature (to obtaining three trials).
13. Place the ball in a box of dry ice and record the temperature of the dry ice, repeat steps 1-6 3 times for this temperature (to obtain three trials).
14. Record the pressure of the ball with a pressure sensor after it has been removed from the dry ice.
15. Record the temperature of the ball with an infrared temperature sensor after it has been removed from the dry ice.
16. Drop it from 1 meter and then repeat steps 12 and 13 3 times (to obtain three trials).

Figure 2: Setup

Safety:

<u>Risks of burns:</u> using water at 60°C and above can cause burns to skin. Using gloves or tongs when placing or removing the ball in the water bath is advisable at these high temperatures to reduce this risk.

<u>Dry Ice:</u> this substance is extremely cold, around -79°C, there always use caution when handling it. Wear gloves and never expose skin directly for a pronlonged perood as this can freeze cells an burn the skin. Also make sure to use the dry ice in a well ventilated room or in a fume cupboard as it gives off a lot of carbond dixide which can be dangerous.

Data collection:

Using Logger Pro, and the videos obtained during the experiment, the values needed to calculate the coefficient of restitution, namely the height at which the ball is dropped and the height the ball bounces, can be extracted. As a meter rule was placed in the shot, this can be used as a scale on Logger Pro as to be able to obtain distance value, an example can be seen in figure 2.

This produces a graph showing the full motion of the ball, both horizontally and vertically (shown in figure 4), however we are only interested in specific values: the drop height (circled in red), the height of the floor (circled in yellow) and the height of the bounce (circled in orange).

This method of collecting data which will be used to calculate the coefficient of restitution, has some limitations. Firstly, the camera used is an iPhone 5 and has a capability of 30fps meaning that if the ball were to have reached its peak and fallen within 1/30 of a second, it would not be recorded by the camera and therefore the peak recorded would be lower than the actual peak. This issue is also faced when determining the floor value as it might reach the floor and bounce back, all within 1/30 of a second and thus would not yield accurate results.

Figure 3: Logger Pro Video Analysis

Another limitation stems from the use of a ruler as a scale. The ruler must be manually highlighted on Logger Pro for a scale to be created but this means that it depends on how exact this manual selection is done. Additionally, the position of the ball is manually denoted, adding a similar problem as above. An uncertainty of ±0.005m is assumed for the ruler itself as this is half of the smallest division but assuming this for the distances generated by Logger Pro is an over simplification as the uncertainty here stems from not only how precisely the scale was selected but also how accurately the positions of the balls were recorded. This being said, there is no comprehensive way of obtaining an accurate uncertainty due to those parameters and thus the uncertainty of ±0.005m will be used in the data analysis.

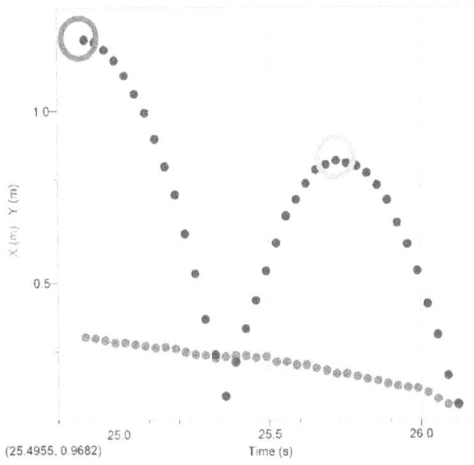

Figure 4: Motion Graph of Ball

Data Processing:

Temperature of Ball T / °C $\Delta T = \pm 2\%$	Drop Height d / m $\Delta d = \pm 0.005m$	Bounce Height b / m $\Delta b = \pm 0.005m$	Floor Height f / m $\Delta f = \pm 0.005m$	Pressure p / kPa $\Delta p = \pm 4\ kPa$
-17	1.346	0.740	0.362	128
-10	1.300	0.688	0.258	129
-10	1.337	0.770	0.312	133
24	1.202	0.782	0.212	140
33	1.204	0.818	0.173	146
49	1.206	0.852	0.167	152
58	1.211	0.882	0.179	156

In this experiment, the coefficient of restitution is what is being studied and thus it must be calculated using the following equation:

$$C_r = \sqrt{\frac{h}{H}}$$

The heights referred to in this equation are not simply the height of the bounce and the height of the drop from the table above, these values must be further refined. The point at which the ball hits the ground should theoretically be 0m but due to the position of the ruler in the video relative to the camera, this value is slightly above 0. This can easily be accounted for by taking the difference of the floor height and the drop height and bounce height respectively. An example calculation and the error which it carries can be seen below:

1) $C_r = \sqrt{\frac{h}{H}}$
 2) Adjusting heights using floor height value:
   a) $h = b - f = 0.882 - 0.179$
   b) $H = d - f = 1.211 - 0.179$
 3) $r = \sqrt{\frac{0.703}{1.032}}$
 4) $r = \sqrt{0.681}$
 5) $r = 0.83$
	Uncertainty Calculations:
	 1. $\Delta h = \Delta H = \Delta d + \Delta f$
	 2. $\Delta h = \Delta H = 0.005 + 0.005$
	 3. $\Delta h = \Delta H = 0.01$
	 4. $\Delta r = \frac{1}{2} \times \left(\frac{\Delta H}{H} + \frac{\Delta h}{h}\right)$
	 5. $\Delta r = \frac{1}{2} \times \left(\frac{0.01}{0.703} + \frac{0.01}{1.032}\right)$
	 6. $\Delta r = \frac{1}{2} \times (0.0142 + 0.00969)$
	 7. $\Delta r = 1.2\% = \pm 0.01$

Performing this calculation across all trials yields the following table and graph with uncertainties[2]:

Temperature of Ball T / °C ΔT = ±2%	Actual Drop Height H / m ΔH = ±0.01m	Actual Bounce Height h / m Δh = ±0.01m	Coefficient of Restitution r Δr = ±0.01
-17	0.98	0.38	0.62
-10	1.04	0.43	0.64
-10	1.03	0.46	0.67
24	0.99	0.57	0.76
33	1.03	0.64	0.79
49	1.04	0.69	0.81
58	1.03	0.70	0.83

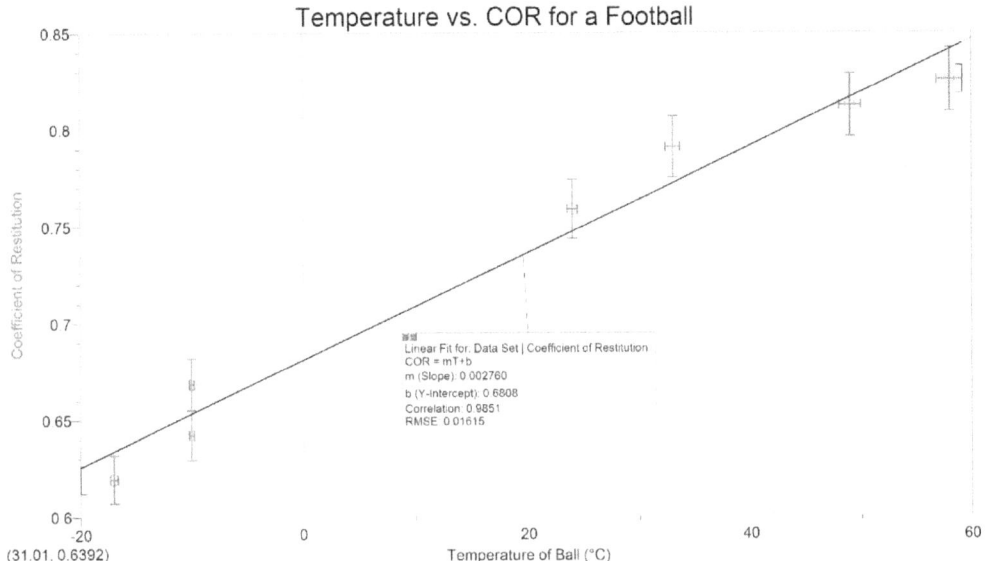

Conclusion:

A linear correlation can be predicted from the data on this graph, despite it not passing through each point, it does pass through the error bars of each point and thus has a relatively high correlation of 0.9851. In terms of the experiment, it is clear that as the temperature of the ball increases, the coefficient of restitution also increases by a fixed value. It was hypothesized that this phenomenon was due to the change in air pressure in the ball. To make sure that the pressure was changing due to temperature by a significant amount, this data was collected during the experiment and can be seen to the right aswell as in graphical form on the next page.

Temperature of Ball T / °C ΔT = ±2%	Pressure p / kPa Δp = ±4 kPa
-17	128
-10	129
-10	133
24	140
33	146
49	152
58	156

---

[2] The uncertainty for the coefficient of restitution had different percentage uncertainties ranging from 1.8% to 1.2% but all the absolute uncertainties were 0.01 so this is what is used for the entire column

The graph does provide the basis for a linear correlation between the pressure inside the ball and the temperature of the ball and this does follow the Ideal Gas Law. Additionally, the graph shows that the pressures do vary significantly with an overall range of 28 kPa. This difference in pressure, caused by exposing the balls to different temperatures, is what causes the balls to bounce at different heights and thus have different coefficients of resitution. The pressure exerts an outwards force which resists the deformation of the ball. The higher pressure will cause the ball to retain it's shape and the colision will therfore take less time allowing for a larger force as $F = \frac{\Delta p}{t}$ and therefore the force exerted by the ball onto the ground is inversely proportional to the time. This force is what allows the ball to bounce and reach different heights each time. The graph above is similar to what was predicted in the background information and thus the hypothesis is correct.

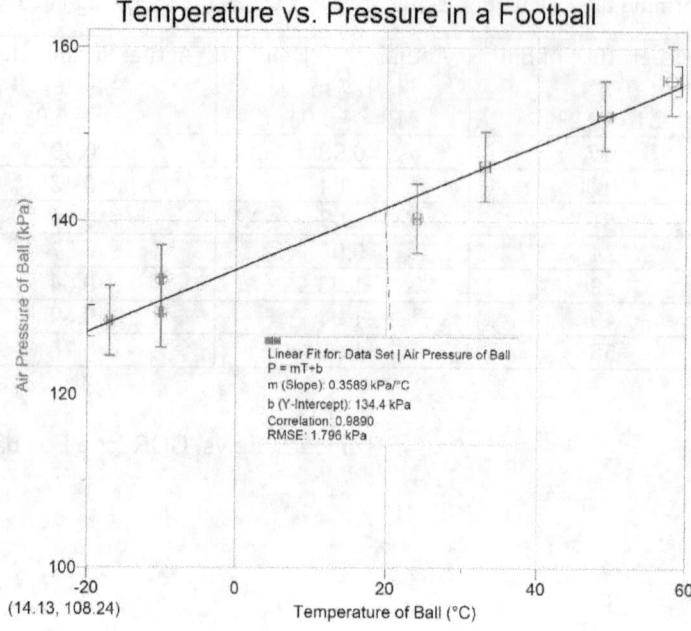

Thus far, this experiment has assumed that it is the pressure inside the hollow ball which is causing a change in the coefficient of resitution where $Coefficient\ of\ Resitution \propto Pressure$. Using the ideal gas law, the pressure and temperature are assumed to be interchanageable in this relationship but, this all relies on the idea that the temperature is only having an affect on the gas inside the ball and not the other physical properties such as the material the ball is made of. This being said, the initially hypothesis could be correct but if a solid ball behaved the same as a hollow ball under the same condititions, this would mean that it is not the pressure which allows for a higher coefficient of resitituion. On the other hand, if the solid ball showed no changes in it's coeffecient of resitution at different temperatures, the conclusion made above would be more substantial and we could predict that the impact of temperature on the material of the ball would have negligible impact on the coefficient of resitution.

Repeating with Solid Balls:

The following data was obtained when a golf ball was used:

Temperature of Ball	Actual Drop Height	Actual Bounce Height	Coefficient of Restitution
T / °C	H / m	h / m	r
T = ±2%	H = ±0.01m	h = ±0.01m	r = ±0.01
-10	0.98	0.69	0.84
-30	1.06	0.60	0.76
23	1.00	0.77	0.87
37	1.01	0.78	0.88
48	1.02	0.80	0.89
60	1.00	0.80	0.90

Here an exponentional fit is more appropriate, yielding a correlation of 0.9964. The correlation is not proportional but as the temperature increases, the coefficient of resitution also increases (just not by a constant value).

The following data was obtained when using a solid rubber ball:

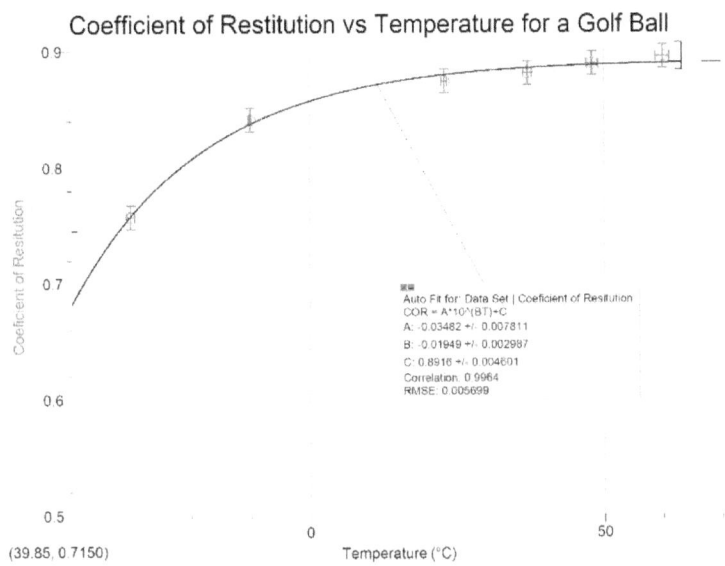

Temperature of Ball	Actual Drop Height	Actual Bounce Height	Coefficient of Restitution
T / °C	H / m	h / m	r
T = ±2%	H = ±0.01m	h = ±0.01m	r = ±0.01
-15	0.98	0.66	0.82
-35	1.08	0.49	0.68
24	1.03	0.76	0.86
38	1.04	0.80	0.88
47	1.03	0.78	0.87
50	1.01	0.79	0.88
62	1.03	0.80	0.88

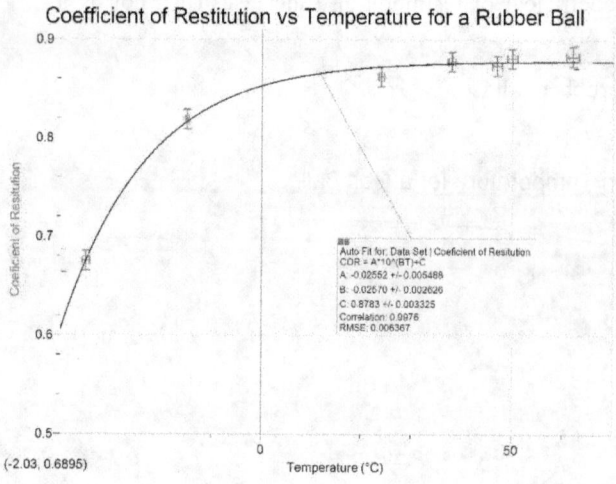

Coefficient of Restitution vs Temperature for a Rubber Ball

Again, an exponential relationship fits the data best, with a correlation value of 0.9976. The fact that these completely different solid balls, have very similar relationships is something to note. Also, these balls which do not have gasses in them like the football still see an increase in their coefficient of resitution when their temperature increases. This signifies that the temperature is having an effect on a different physical property other than the gas inside the ball. The relationship between these quantitites however, is different. With the football, we saw a linear graph while here, an exponetial one seems obvious. This is due to the effect of temperature on the material of the ball on a microscopic scale. The lower tempertures will cause the bonds in the material to strengthen as some crystalization takes place. The stronger bonds cause the material to be more rigid and thus it is harder to deform.[3]

In our intial hypothesis, the more rigid ball would bounce higher but here, it behaves in the opposite way. Thas is because the nature of the collision is different. As the ball is not hollow, the ability for it to retain it's energy relies on it deforming slightly. In figure 5 this is demonstrated, if the ball cannot deform at all, then the energy will be dissipated through sound and heat and won't allow for a bounce. If the ball loses it's shape too much, it will not be able to return to it's original position and thus will have a lower coefficient of restitution. With a football slight deformation will happen regardless as the material is flexible and the ball is hollow, but with a solid ball, if the ball is too rigid throughout, it will not significantly deform and thus will not be able to retain it's energy on colision.

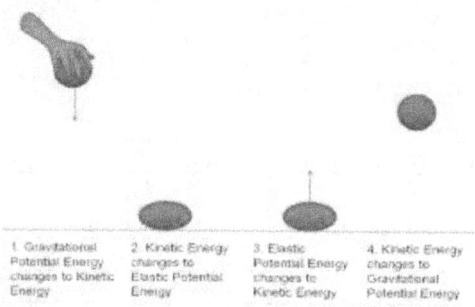

Figure 5: Ball Deforming

This means that at lower temperatures, more rigid balls will actually lead to lower coefficients of restitution. At higher temperatures, the intermolecular bonds will weaken and the reverse will happen. However, the increases in temperature at higher temperatures cause much smaller changes in the coefficient of resitution compared to changes at lower temperatures. This is because, when the materials are at high temperatures, it is solely the looser intermolecular bonds which cause the flexibility of the material. But, at low temeperatures, usually lower than -2°C for rubber,[4] the material begins to crystalize. This crystallization has a much greater effect on the rigidness of the material and for this reason, lower temperatures cause drastic differences in the coefficient of restitution compared to higher temperatures.

---

[3] Russell, E. W. "The Crystallization of Vulcanized Natural Rubber at Low Temperatures." *Rubber Chemistry and Technology* 25.3 (1952): 397-411. Web.

[4] Russell, E. W. "The Crystallization of Vulcanized Natural Rubber at Low Temperatures." *Rubber Chemistry and Technology* 25.3 (1952): 397-411. Web.

Improvements:

Multiple Trials:

A major limitation of this experiment was the fact that repeat trials were not done. As it took longer for the water baths to change the temperature of the balls, there was not enough time for repeat trials. If this was taken into consideration and there had been enough time for multiple trials, then average could have been taken and thus more accurate graphs could be drawn. Additionally, having repeat trials would allow for more accurate uncertainties calculated by using the range of the repeat trials. Unfortunately, due to time limitations the results obtained and the analysis derived is not entirely accurate.

Temperature of the Ball:

The input variable was the temperature so this was arguably the most important factor to control and record during the experiment. However, as these balls were being removed from the water baths before being dropped to record their temperature and their pressure, heat was being lost to the surroundings. One way of reducing this heat loss would be to assume that the temperature of the water baths and that of the balls is equal as this would drastically reduce the time during which the ball is exposed and thus allow more heat to be retained. The graph below shows the relationship between temperature and coefficient of resitiution but this time instead of using the temperature of the ball, the temperature of the water bath is used:

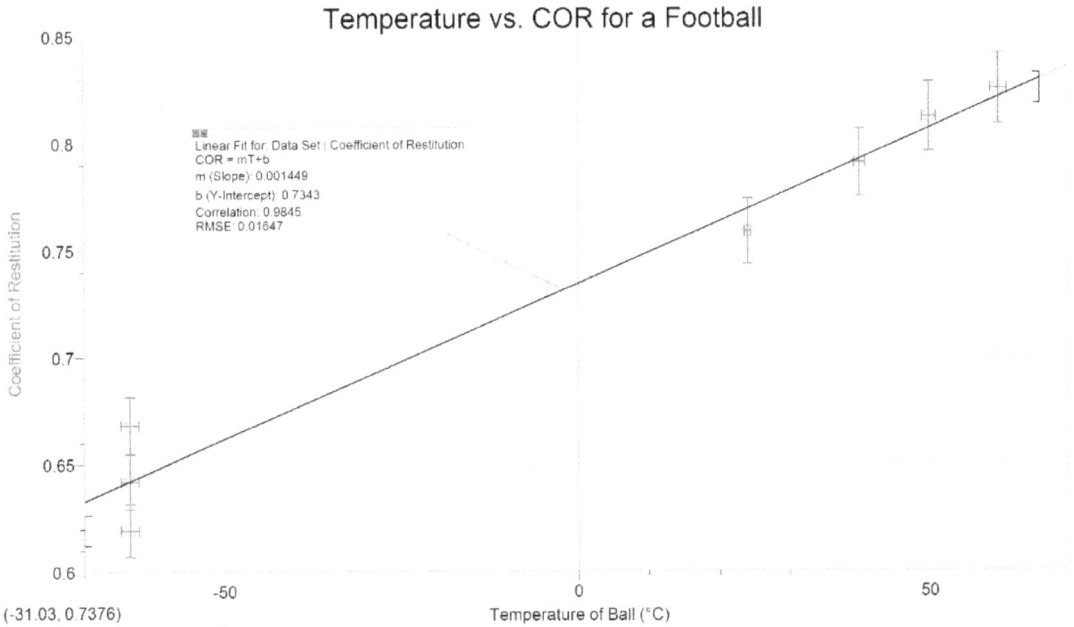

This graph, using the new improved method, does still pose some problems. Firstly, the correlation value is actually slightly lower than in the original graph (0.9845 vs. 0.9851). The more significant issue however, is the fact that three data points, all collected by exposing the balls to dry ice at -63.5°C, give different values for the coefficient of restitution. The reason for this is clear, not only were the balls not exposed for the same exact time, but also, when repeating the experiment, the ball would become even colder as it was placed back into the dry ice. For this reason, it is probably advisable to stick with the original method.

Another way this could be fixed would be by leaving the balls in their respective water baths for longer periods of time. Despite not being recorded, the balls were left in the baths for approximately 10 minutes each time, if this was increased to 1 hour, the balls would probably reach thermal equilibrium with the liquids. This would allow for the temperatures of the water baths to be used as data without skewing the results.

Measuring Distance:

To measure the height the ball was falling and bouncing, a camera was used with a ruler. Using LoggerPro, this setup can be converted to useful values. However, this method has three major weaknesses. Firstly, the position of the camera relative to the experment can cause problems. If the camera is at an angle, it will distort the preceived motion of the ball and yield false values. Secondly, this method relies heavily on users inputing the length of the ruler and the position of the ball. As it is done by a human, it is not the most precise method and can cause large variations if done carelessely. The last limitation of this method is the fact that the camera is only 30fps, this means that whatever is happening at a more precise resolution is not caputred.

A different method of measuring the distance, which would circumvent all the aforementioned issues, is the use of a motion detector. This does not rely on any visual interface and instead has ultrasonic capabilities. It would yield more precise and accurate results and not need any human involvement to extract the data.

Conclusion:

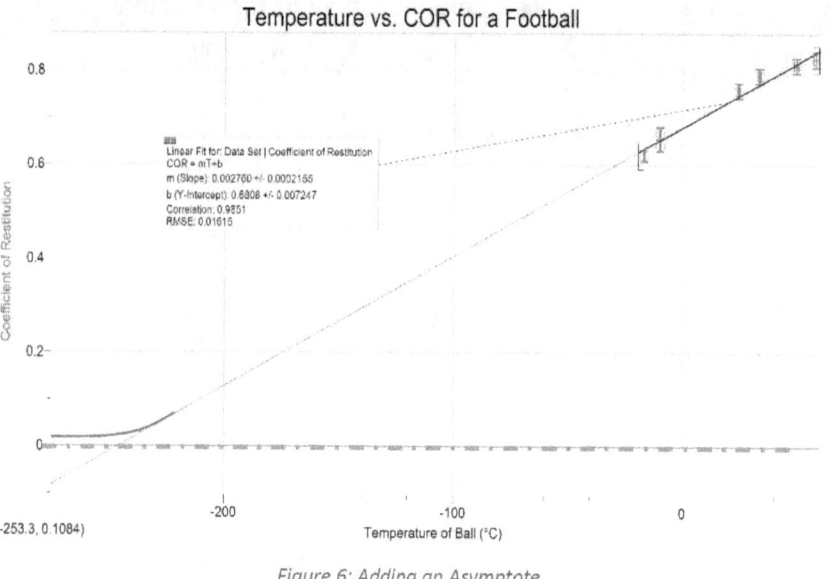

Figure 6: Adding an Asymptote

Overall, it is clear than for any of the ball types tested, an increase in temperature would cause an increase in the coefficient of resitution. In the football this is due to pressure while in the solid balls, this is due to the materials' properties. For all ball types, the graphs had lines of best fit which would reach 0 and cross the x-axis thus signifying a negative coefficient of restituiton. A coefficient of restitution of 0 is impossible as this would mean that no energy was kept after the first bounce. A coefficient of restitution of less than 0 is even more outlandish as the square root sign in the formula forbids it. Also, this would mean that the ball would actually have a negative bounce height or drop height another impossibility. This means that it must trail off and inherently, it can come close to zero, but can never reach it and definetly can never pass it. This would call for an assymptote as shown in figure 6. Having an asymptote could lead us to believe that the entire function is different an thus an extension could entail furthur testing at extremely low temperatures. This would allow us to know if the relationship between coefficient of resitituion and temperature keeps it's linear characterisitcs at extremely low temperatures.

Despite the experiment having focus on footballs, repeating it with the solid balls did add some information about footballs. The golf and rubber balls did have a relationship between the coefficient of resitution and the temperature but it was not constant, suggesting an exponential relationship. For footballs, which would have similar properties on a miscroscopic scale, this could suggest that the effect of the temperature on the coefficient of resitution is not only linked to the gas pressure but also to the material used. This might mean that the effect of temperature on the coefficient of restitution is caused mostly by the properties of the gas at hight temperatures, above 30°C. For lower temperatures, below 0°C, the changes in the coefficient of resitution could be attributed to the microscopic properties of the material.

Works Cited

Haron, Adli, and K. A. Ismail. "Coefficient of Restitution of Sports Balls: A Normal Drop Test." *IOP Conference Series: Materials Science and Engineering* 36.1 (2012): n. pag. Web. 7 May 2016. <http://iopscience.iop.org/article/10.1088/1757-899X/36/1/012038/pdf>.

Newton, Isaac, Alexandre Koyre, and I. Bernard Cohen. *Philosophiae Naturalis Principia Mathematica: The Third Edition (1726) with Variant Readings*. Cambridge: Cambridge U, 1972. Print.

Russell, E. W. "The Crystallization of Vulcanized Natural Rubber at Low Temperatures." Rubber Chemistry and Technology 25.3 (1952): 397-411. Web.

5. HOW DOES THE MASS OF THE COUNTERWEIGHT USED TO LAUNCH THE PROJECTILE OF FIXED MASS AFFECT THE RANGE OF THE PROJECTILE?

INTRODUCTION

Catapults are ancient Roman weapons that launch projectiles at their enemies using a large weight to project it. Earlier in the year, I had to build a catapult during a leadership camp as part of a team building activity. Though we added an object of very large counterweight to project a projectile of very small mass, the object did not fly as far as expected. However, one of the other groups used a less heavy counterweight and their projectile flew further. This made me want to investigate the effect of the mass of the weight to the range of the projectile.

RESEARCH QUESTION

To investigate the relationship, I came up with my research question. "**How does the mass of the counterweight used to launch the projectile of fixed mass affect the range of the projectile?**" I will be investigating the effect on a projectile of fixed mass so as to be able to establish a relationship based on just two variables, so that a future trend can be predicted.

Independent Variable: The mass of the counterweight used to launch the projectile, defined as M_c. An electronic mass balance will be used to measure the pieces of plasticine used as the counterweight. The range of masses will be from 400 g to 850 g in 50 g intervals.

Dependent Variable: The range of the projectile, measured by recording the initial point of landing on the floor after the projectile is launched to the point from which it was launched. *(See diagram 1 for the labeled diagram of catapult.)*

Controlled Variables: *(See diagram 1 for the labeled diagram of catapult.)*
1. Mass of the projectile, controlled by using the same projectile of (100±1) g throughout the experiment. Controlled so that the relationship is strictly between the mass of the counterweight and the range.
2. Height of catapult, controlled by using the same catapult. Controlled because the initial height of launch will affect the range.
3. Height of pivot, controlled by using the same catapult. Controlled because the initial height of launch will affect the range.

4. Initial angle of launch, calculated to be 57.1°, controlled by using the same catapult. Controlled because the initial angle of launch will affect the range.
5. Initial distance between the projectile and the pivot, controlled by using the same projectile. Controlled because a change in the distance will affect the moment about the pivot, which will in turn affect the force with which the projectile is launched and hence, the range.
6. Distance between the counterweight holder and the pivot, controlled by using the same catapult. Controlled because a change in the distance will affect the moment about the pivot, which will in turn affect the force with which the projectile is launched and hence, the range.
7. Air resistance, controlled by conducting the experiment in the same place with the fans off and the windows closed. Controlled because wind on the projectile will affect the range.

THEORY

Levers

A catapult falls under one of three classes of levers, specifically to the first class of levers, the type where the fulcrum or pivot is placed in between the load and the effort, in this case the projectile and the counterweight.[1] Due to the position of the load and effort, they will move in opposite directions about the pivot. This will cause a change in the net moment about the pivot when the mass of either objects or the distance of the objects from the pivot changes. The moment about the pivot can be calculated through the equation (Moment) = (Force) x (Distance from Pivot). In the case of this catapult, the projectile and counterweights are equidistant from the pivot and hence, the moment about the pivot is determined solely by the force at either end, (since the mass of the ruler and the support beam is constant, and the pivot is in the middle of the ruler for this setup).

Forces and Energy Conversion

The force can be calculated to be a product of the mass and the acceleration, which in this case is the acceleration due to gravity, a constant that is equal to 9.81 m s^{-2}. Since the

---

[1] "Design and Technology. Mechanisms." *BBC Bitesized*. BBC, n.d. Web. 5 May 2016.
<http://www.bbc.co.uk/schools/gcsebitesize/design/systemscontrol/mechanismsrev1.shtml>.

acceleration is constant for both the masses, and since it will not affect the horizontal velocity and hence will not affect the range of the projectile, the force is dependent on the mass of the object. It can be seen that the moment about the pivot is dependent on the mass of the counter weight since the mass of the projectile is also constant. Therefore, in this specific case based on the class of the lever and the design of the catapult, the mass of the counterweight must always be greater than the mass of the projectile launched. It is generally assumed that with an increase in the mass of the counterweight for the same projectile, the range of the projectile will also increase. With a larger mass of the counterweight, there will be a larger net momentum, resulting in a higher initial velocity of the projectile. But is there a maximum limit to the increase in range? After a certain point, the range may begin to decrease again. Can the maximum range of the projectile be found to optimize the mass of the counterweight?

Newton's Laws of Motion

According to Newton's First Law, the horizontal velocity of the projectile will be constant since there is no horizontal external force exerted on it, assuming that there is negligible air resistance, and hence, the range will not be affected. According to Newton's second law, there will be a constant force exerted on the vertical component of the velocity of the projectile due to the constant acceleration. With a combination of these two components, we see that the projectile will be launched and follow a parabolic path on the air. Using kinematics equations, the range of the projectile can be calculated based on the initial velocity of the projectile.

The equation used is:

$$y = y_0 + (\tan(90 - \theta))x - \left(\frac{\frac{g}{2}}{v_0^2 (\cos(90-\theta))^2}\right)x^2 \qquad \text{(Equation 1)}$$

Where,

y = The height of the projectile at any moment, measured in meters, m.

y_0 = The initial height of the projectile at the moment of launch, measured in meters, m.

θ = The angle between the arm of the catapult and the floor, calculated by using trigonometric rations of the height of the pivot off the ground and it's distance from the initial position of the projectile before launch, represented in degrees, °.

x = The range of the projectile, measured in meters, m.

g = The acceleration due to gravity gravitational, 9.81 m s^{-2}.

v_0 = The initial velocity of the projectile at the moment of launch, measured in meters per second, m s^{-1}.

The equation above resembles a quadratic equation, so as to represent the parabolic nature of the motion of the projectile.

However, the motion of the projectile can also be explained through equations relating to energy conservation in the closed system. The energy gained of the projectile launched will be equal to the net energy lost from the counterweight when it is released, assuming that there is no friction in the system.

The gravitational potential energy lost from the counterweight can be calculated through the equation:

$E_1 = M_c \times g \times \Delta h$

Where,

M_c = The mass of the counterweight, measured in kilograms, kg.
g = The acceleration due to gravity gravitational, 9.81 m s^{-2}.
Δh = The height of the counterweight launcher from the ground, measured in meters, m.

The energy gained by the projectile can be calculated through the following equation:

$E_2 = (M_p \times g \times \Delta h) + ((1/2) \times M_p \times v_0^2) + ((1/2) \times M_c \times v_0^2)$

Where,

M_p = The mass of the projectile, measured in kilograms, kg.
g = The acceleration due to gravity gravitational, 9.81 m s^{-2}.
Δh = The height of the projectile launcher from the ground, measured in meters, m.
M_c = The mass of the counterweight measured in kilograms, kg.
v_0 = The initial velocity of the projectile at the moment of launch, measured in meters per second, m s^{-1}. The velocity of the projectile as it gains KE will be the same as the velocity of the counterweight as it loses GPE because of the fact that they are both equidistant from the pivot.

It can be assumed that the energy of the system is conserved, $E_1 = E_2$, ignoring rotational kinetic energy and assuming that the masses moved vertically.

Therefore, we can equate the equations to get:

$$M_c \times g \times \Delta h = (M_p \times g \times \Delta h) + ((1/2) \times M_p \times v_0^2) + ((1/2) \times M_c \times v_0^2) \qquad \text{(Equation 2)}$$

Equation 2 can be used to find the initial velocity of the projectile based on the conservation of energy. This value can then be substituted into Equation 1 to find the theoretical value of the range of the projectile.

The graph of the range of the projectile against the mass of the counterweight is expected to be a straight line due to the fact that it is directly proportional to the initial velocity of the projectile, which should increase with an increase in the mass of the counterweight.

METHODOLOGY

Pre-Trial Setup

The catapult was designed and built so that the mass of both the projectile as well as the counterweight would be easy to change. Also it would be easy to measure the range of the projectile thus, increasing the accuracy of the readings. The basic design of the catapult was adapted[2]. I then adapted it to a smaller scale lab version that allowed me to easily change the mass of the counterweight and measure the range.

Apparatus to build the catapult:

1 x Meter rule

2 x Retort stands and clamps

1 x 1.50 Meter long wooden pole

2 x Ladles (used as launchers)

Raffia string

Masking tape

1 x Plastic tube (for pivot)

1 x Spirit level

1 x 1.50 Meter long measuring tapes

Procedure to build the catapult:

---

[2] "Catapult." *Brill's New Pauly* (n.d.): n. pag. Web. 6 May 2016. <http://www.latech.edu/latechstep/p/pc/pmm.pdf>.

Two retort stands were set up with clamps that were fixed to be exactly 1 meter off the ground. The pole was then clamped on and held up by the retort stand. A spirit level was used to make sure that the pole was parallel to the ground. The meter rule was then tied onto the pole using raffia string. Unfortunately, this created a lot of friction between the meter rule and the pole and did not allow the motion of the meter rule about the pole to be smooth.

I then decided to slit a thin plastic tube, made from slicing off the end of a small cylindrical box, onto the pole before re-clamping its edges onto the retort stands. However, while moving the catapult while using the spirit level, the pole slipped off. The pole was then re-clamped such that 10 cm of the edge of the pole on either side protruded, thus securing a firmer grip on it. The measuring tape was then used to mark out the center of the pole and the center of the tube, and tape was used on either end of the tube to tape the pole, such that the pole's horizontal movement was restricted and it could not move from the center of the pole, but it was still able to rotate freely.

The raffia string was then used to tie the meter rule to the center of the tube. The 50.0 cm mark was tied to the center, so as to ensure that the masses would be equidistant to the pivot. The ladles were then taped onto either end of the meter rule such that only the curved edge was protruding. The spirit level was then used again to make sure that the meter rule was at the center of the pole and that the pole was still parallel to the ground. The labeled diagram below shows the entire catapult set-up after it was built.

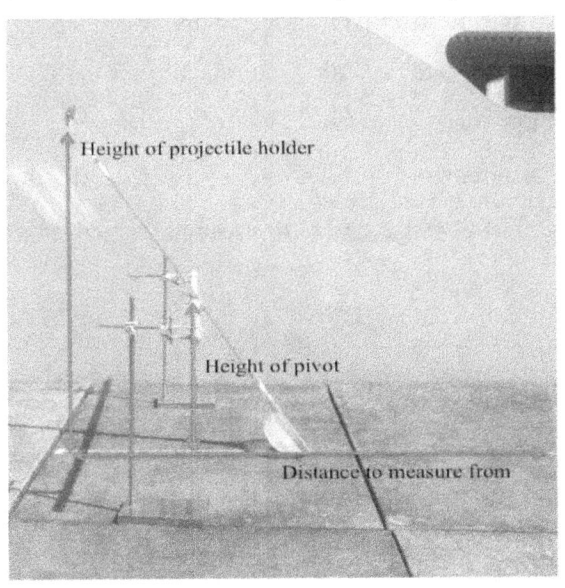 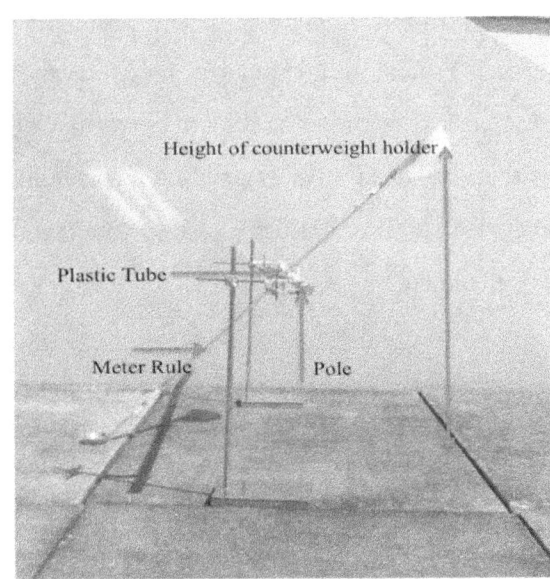

Diagram 1: Labeled diagram of the Catapult

To carry out the experiment

Apparatus for the experiment:

2 x 1.50 Meter long measuring tapes Plasticine
1 x Electronic mass balance Thin plastic bags
Nylon String

Procedure for the experiment:

The plasticine was split into small bags and placed into 11 separate thin plastic bags. The mass of each bag was measured using an electronic mass balance and then the amount of plasticine in the bag was adjusted to get the desired mass. The masses measured were 100g, 400g, 450g, 500g, 550g, 600g, 650g, 700g, 750g, 800g and 850g. Each bag was then tied such that the bag did not unravel and it kept its spherical shape. The masses were then re-measured, and a bit of the edge of each of the bags were cut off to account for the mass of the string, such that the new mass with the string was still the originally desired mass. The catapult was then placed ready on the floor such that the counterweight holder was placed on the ground. A mass was suspended from a piece of string that was held up to the projectile launcher. The point at which the mass touches the ground was marked out using a piece of tape to be position of launch as can be seen from the diagram above, so that the range can be measured from there. The measuring tapes were taped onto the floor from that point to the front of the catapult where the projectile would land. The meter rule on the catapult was then adjusted such that the projectile launcher was on the floor. The 100 g projectile was placed into the launcher. The 400 g plasticine ball was then placed into the counterweight launcher and the position of landing of the projectile was measured and recorded. This was then repeated 3 more times and the range of the projectile with a 400 g counterweight was measured and recorded, and an average of the readings was calculated. The 100 g projectile was then launched 4 times with counterweights of different masses. The masses were 450g, 500g, 550g, 600g, 650g, 700g, 750g, 800g and 850g. The average range for these masses was also calculated.

A graph of average range against mass of the counterweight was plotted. An equation for the regression curve was obtained along with its R^2 coefficient.

Safety Precautions:

During the making of the catapult, there were a lot of safety issues that needed to be taken into account. Firstly, the pole was sawed down on either end and then, it had to be smoothened for an even surface. The plastic tube also had to be sawed down and sanded at both ends to prevent any injuries from the sharp edges. During this process, there could have been potential risks while using the saw and sanding machine and hence, cautions were taken. Gloves, goggles and closed toe shoes were worn to prevent any injuries from splinters. Furthermore, when actually using the catapult, there could be potential injuries caused by the flying projectile. It is therefore important to carry out the experiment in a closed location that is empty, so that no one gets hurt.

DATA COLLECTION AND PROCESSING

The experiment was carried out and a set of raw data was obtained.

Table 1. Table of Raw and Processed Data

Mass of counterweight, M_c /kg	$Range_1$, X_1 /m	$Range_2$, X_2 /m	$Range_3$, X_3 /m	$Range_4$, X_4 /m	$Range_{average}$, X_{avg} /m	$\Delta Range_{avg}$ of projectile/m
$\Delta mass = \pm 0.001g$	\multicolumn{4}{c}{$\Delta Range = \pm 0.01m$}			
0.400	1.58	1.61	1.60	1.62	1.60	0.02
0.450	1.70	1.72	1.74	1.71	1.72	0.02
0.500	1.86	1.84	1.89	1.90	1.87	0.03
0.550	1.94	1.97	1.93	1.94	1.95	0.02
0.600	2.00	1.98	1.99	1.96	1.98	0.02
0.650	1.94	1.92	1.90	1.91	1.92	0.02
0.700	1.85	1.88	1.86	1.84	1.86	0.02
0.750	1.68	1.70	1.72	1.71	1.70	0.02
0.800	1.57	1.59	1.60	1.58	1.59	0.02
0.850	1.47	1.48	1.46	1.49	1.48	0.02

Justification of Uncertainties

1. ΔMass = 0.001kg. The precision of the electronic mass balance is 0.1g, but it fluctuated at 0.0001kg, so 0.001kg was taken instead.
2. ΔRange = ±0.01 m. Due to large diameter of the plasticine ball launched, the precision up to which the range can be measured to is 0.01m.
3. ΔRange$_{average}$ of projectile = Difference between maximum range or the minimum range (whichever is larger) from the average range.

The following graph was obtained by plotting Range of the projectile against the Mass of the counterweight.

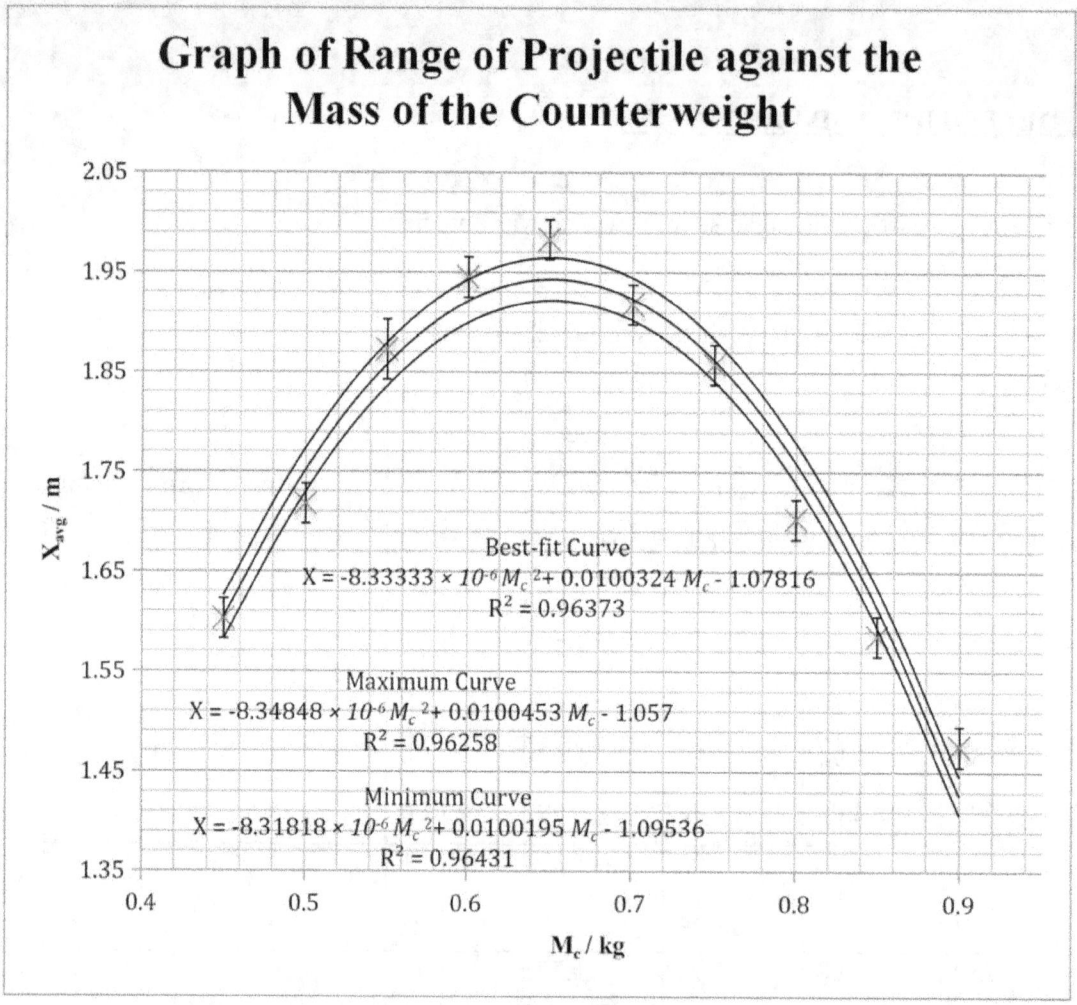

A quadratic equation was obtained and plotted with the equation Range = -8.33333 × $10^{-6} M_c^2$ + 0.0100324 M_c - 1.07816. The R^2 value was calculated to be 0.964 (3.s.f.). Using the square of the regression value for the curve, the error can be calculated. The error for the graph of mass ratio against range can be calculated as $\frac{1-0.964}{1}$ × 100% = 3.6%. Since the error for the graph is less than 5%, we can consider the value obtained from the graph precise. The maximum and minimum values of the range were obtained by adding and subtracting the uncertainty from the measured value. These values then plotted against the mass of the counterweight. The uncertainty of the counterweight was not plotted as it is the independent variable, and it has a relatively small uncertainty, as can be seen from the error bars.

Due to the parabolic nature of the curve, it can be concluded that there is an optimum mass of the counterweight for the maximum range for a projectile of fixed mass. This can be calculated by looking at the mass that corresponds to the maximum range, which is the turning point on the graph.

For the Best-Fit curve:

$X = -8.33333 \times 10^{-6} M_c^2 + 0.0100324 M_c - 1.07816$

Differentiate both sides with respect to M_c:

$\frac{\partial X}{\partial Mc} = -1.6666666 \times 10^{-5} Mc + 0.0100324$

Equate to zero to find the mass of the counterweight with maximum range.

$-1.6666666 \times 10^{-5} Mc + 0.0100324 = 0$

$Mc = 0.601944 \, kg$

$= 0.602 \, kg \, (3.s.f.)$

Therefore the range, $X = 1.94 \, m$

For the Maximum-Curve:

$X = -8.34848 \times 10^{-6} M_c^2 + 0.0100453 M_c - 1.057$

Differentiate both sides with respect to M_c:

$\frac{\partial X}{\partial Mc} = -1.669696 \times 10^{-5} Mc + 0.0100453$

Equate to zero to find the mass of the counterweight with maximum range.

$-1.669696 \times 10^{-5} Mc + 0.0100453 = 0$

$Mc = 0.601624 \, kg$

$= 0.602 \, kg \, (3.s.f.)$

Therefore the maximum range, $X = 1.96 \, m$

For the Minimum-Curve:

$X = -8.31818 \times 10^{-6} M_c^2 + 0.0100195 M_c - 1.09536$

Differentiate both sides with respect to M_c:

$\frac{\partial X}{\partial Mc} = -1.663636 \times 10^{-5} Mc + 0.0100195$

Equate to zero to find the mass of the counterweight with maximum range.

$-1.663636 \times 10^{-5} Mc + 0.0100195 = 0$

$Mc = 0.602265 \, kg$

$= 0.602 \, kg \, (3.s.f.)$

Therefore the minimum range, $X = 1.92 \, m$

Since the maximum range for the maximum curve and minimum curve have the same mass of the counterweight as that of the best-fit curve, it can be concluded that the optimal mass of the counterweight for a 0.100 kg projectile is 0.602 kg. The range achieved with this mass is (1.94 ± 0.002) m.

It can be seen that this curve does not fit the trend proposed by the original equations 1 and 2, and hence, further analysis is required. From the first two equations, the theoretical range of the projectile with a 0.602 kg counterweight can be calculated and hence, compared to the value found on the graph.

We can first substitute values into Equation 2 to find the theoretical initial velocity squared:

$$M_c \times g \times \Delta h = (M_p \times g \times \Delta h) + ((1/2) \times M_p \times v_0^2) + ((1/2) \times M_c \times v_0^2)$$

$$(0.602)(9.81)(0.84) = (0.1)(9.81)(1.11) + ((1/2)(0.1)(v_0^2) + ((1/2)(0.602)(v_0^2))$$

$$v_0^2 = 11.0308 \text{ m}^2 \text{ s}^{-2}$$

$$v_0^2 = 11.0 \text{ m}^2 \text{ s}^{-2} \text{ (3.s.f.)}$$

From here, we can substitute this value into Equation 1 to find the theoretical range:

$$y = y_0 + (\tan(90 - \theta))x - \left(\frac{\frac{g}{2}}{v_0^2 (\cos(90 - \theta))^2}\right)x^2$$

Let y, the height of the catapult at any point, is zero because that is the maximum range.

$$0 = 1.11 + (\tan(90 - 57.1))x - \left(\frac{\frac{9.81}{2}}{11.0308(\cos(90-57.1))^2}\right)x^2$$

$$X = 1.933075726$$

$$X = 1.93 \text{ m (3.s.f.)}$$

From this value, the percentage error can be calculated as $\frac{1.93-1.94}{1.93} \times 100\% = 0.515\ \%$ deviation from the theoretical value. Thus, it can be concluded that, due to the extremely low percentage error, the experimental conclusions are accurate.

CONCLUSION AND EVALUATION

A graph of the range of a projectile of fixed mass against the mass of the counterweight was plotted and a quadratic curve was obtained. During the team building activity, when I first started hypothesizing about the relationship, I assumed that with a heavier counterweight, the range would be further, but that wasn't the case. This investigation shows that the range of the projectile has a maximum value based on the relationship between the mass of the projectile and counterweight. This went against the theory that there should be a linear relationship between the range of the projectile and the mass of the counterweight due to the increased initial velocity. That being said, the percentage error for the maximum range of the projectile was very low and hence the range was accurate. However, the values of the range after the mass of 0.602 kg go against the trend and hence, only the increasing portion of the curve can be considered somewhat accurate.

Strengths and Weaknesses

The experimental procedure was effective in achieving the results to answer the research question. The use of the catapult to measure the range was effective till the maximum measured range and followed the theoretical value very closely. Therefore, the results, being reliable to a certain extent, can be used for further investigation within the field. However the physical structure of this particular catapult limited the accuracy of all the results. This restricts the reliability of the entire set of data, specifically the range measured after the maximum point. Thus, the structure needs to be improved for more accurate results.

There are also some sources of error in this experiment, which could have contributed to the fact that the graph does not follow the theoretical trend.

Sources of Error

1. One major contribution to the random error is in the design of the catapult. The arm of the catapult is made using a meter rule that has ladles at either end and is tied to the pivot using raffia string. When the weight of the counterweight increases, the rotational moment around the pivot increases as well. However, the meter rule has a very small width and is not very thick and hence, the increase in the rotational

moment causes the ruler to bend. Therefore, the angle at which the projectile is launched is not consistent. This affected the range since the initial velocity was also affected. This also resulted in the arm launching the projectile to flip a little, hence affect the angle of launch and thus, affecting the range.

2. Another major error is the lack of precision in the measuring instruments during the calibration of the catapult and masses and in the measurement of the range of the projectile. This will cause a large random error in the each value and hence, the overall accuracy of the results will be affected.

3. The presence of friction in the pivot also restrict the motion of the arm of the catapult and hence, the initial velocity of the projectile will be reduced and hence, so will the range of the projectile. This will result in there being a large systematic and random error.

4. The catapult also does not always fire the projectile in a straight line along the line of the measuring tape. This will affect the measured range of the projectile and hence, also contribute to the random error of the value.

Reduction of Errors to increase Accuracy

1. A wider and thicker plank of wood can be used for the arm of the catapult so as to minimize the bending of the plank with the increase in the rotational momentum of the pivot. Alternatively, a stiffer material can be used to construct the catapult. This will minimize the reduction of the initial velocity of the projectile and hence the range of the projectile will also be more accurate.

2. The angle between the arm of the catapult and the floor was measured using a protractor. To make this angle more precise, the height of the catapult and the length of the arm can be used to find the angle through trigonometry to increase the accuracy of the angle and hence the calculated initial velocity. Furthermore, the mass of the projectile and the counterweights can be measured to a higher precision so as to reduce the error caused by the mass ratio. Also, the range of the projectile was measured by eye and hence, the measured angle may not always be extremely accurate. To fix this, a data logger can be used to record the motion of the catapult and then software can be used to pinpoint the range of the catapult to a much higher accuracy.

3. A small plastic tube was placed around the pole to reduce the initial friction of the catapult. However, there was still friction due to the tape at the side to keep it from sliding as well as the friction between the wooden pole and the inside of the plastic tube. Proper metal spikes can be nailed in at either end of the pole around the tube so as to reduce the friction. Also, the pole and the inside of the tube can also be made to be extremely smooth to minimize friction. Also, a little bit of oil or Vaseline can be rubbed on the inside of the tube to reduce the friction and hence, reduce the error of the initial velocity of the projectile.
4. With a thicker plank, the movement of the arm around the pivot will be better and hence the projectile will also move straighter. Also, the measuring tape can be made into a radius around the catapult so that the angular range can be measured and then resolved to find the horizontal range and hence, the value will be more accurate.

Extension

With the improvements in the experiment and the construction of the catapult so as to reduce the major procedural errors, the experiment can also be carried out for projectiles of different masses.

The experiment can also be carried out using projectiles of different masses to see if the relationship holds. Though the equations used show that the results should resemble a straight line, the new results will most likely follow the same quadratic shape since the same catapult should be used. The maximum point on each of the graphs can be compared and a relationship can be found between the mass ratio of the mass of the projectile and the counterweight and the mass of the counterweight, and the maximum range achieved.

Bibliography

Lucas, Stephen, Salters Horners, and A2 Physics Coursework. *What Affects the Range of a Trebuchet?* (n.d.): n. pag. Web. 1 Apr. 2016.

Krummell, Russell. *THE MATH BEHIND THE MACHINE ANSWER KEY* (n.d.): n. pag. Web. 1 Apr. 2016.

Data Booklet. Risley: BNFL, Information Services Directorate, 1992. Web. 1 Apr. 2016.

"Catapult Physics." *Real World Physics Problems*. N.p., n.d. Web. 01 Apr. 2016. <http://www.real-world-physics-problems.com/catapult-physics.html>.

"Rotational Inertia - Physics Video by Brightstorm." *Rotational Inertia - Physics Video by Brightstorm*. N.p., n.d. Web. 01 Apr. 2016. <https://www.brightstorm.com/science/physics/circular-motion-and-rotational-mechanics/rotational-inertia/>.

"Kinematic Equations." *Kinematic Equations*. N.p., n.d. Web. 01 Apr. 2016. <http://www.physicsclassroom.com/class/1DKin/Lesson-6/Kinematic-Equations>.

"Catapult." *Brill's New Pauly* (n.d.): n. pag. Web. 6 May 2016. <http://www.latech.edu/latechstep/p/pc/pmm.pdf>.

"Design and Technology. Mechanisms." *BBC Bitesized*. BBC, n.d. Web. 5 May 2016. <http://www.bbc.co.uk/schools/gcsebitesize/design/systemscontrol/mechanismsrev1.shtml>.

"Three Lever Classes." *By Ron Kurtus*. N.p., n.d. Web. 06 May 2016. <http://www.school-for-champions.com/machines/levers_classess.htm#.Vyr2waN96Rt>.

"Wolfram|Alpha: Computational Knowledge Engine." *Wolfram|Alpha: Computational Knowledge Engine*. N.p., n.d. Web. 06 May 2016. <http://www.wolframalpha.com/>.

6. STANDING WAVES AND THE EFFECT OF TEMPERATURE ON THE CLARINET

I am a clarinettist and so any scientific study of the sounds that instruments make is significant to me. I was interested in the physics behind musical instruments and decided to combine previous study of standing waves in closed pipes with an investigation into different wavelengths that can be played on the clarinet. I wanted to get fully involved in the experimentation procedure myself by both playing my clarinet and recording results. I also decided to expand on this by investigating the effect that temperature has on the frequency of notes on the clarinet. There are lots of rumours in the musical world that heating or cooling your instrument to different temperatures can have a disastrous effect on pitch and thus can cause tuning issues. I was keen to find out whether this was just rumour or whether I could support it with evidence from experimentation.

Part 1: Standing waves on the clarinet

Contextual information

Standing waves occur in the clarinet pipe when it is being played and air vibrates inside (Wolfe, 2002). The clarinet works by changing the length of the air channel – covering and uncovering its holes. The pitch of the sound produced is dependent on the frequency (The Physics Classroom), and since the equation for frequency relates to wavelength and speed, one of these two qualities must change in order for the pitch of a note on the clarinet to alter. The speed of sound waves is a constant at 340.29 m s^{-1} (Holloway, 2006), so this means that the wavelength changes.

There is a pressure node at the closed end of the clarinet and an antinode at the open end. At the bell of the clarinet, the pressure is around the same value as the pressure outside the clarinet – this means that the acoustic pressure is approximately zero because there is little or no variation in pressure due to sound waves between the two environments (Wolfe, 2002). At the mouthpiece, the pressure is at its highest value.

Thinking of this in graphical terms, the distance between zero and a maximum on a sine graph, or the distance between a node and an antinode, is $\frac{1}{4}$ of a wavelength (Wolfe, 2002). This means that the longest complete standing wave inside the clarinet must have a wavelength of 4 times the length of the instrument (Holloway, 2006).

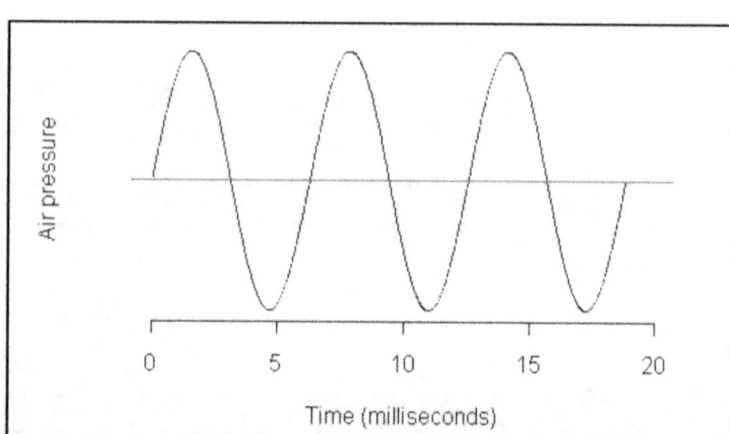

(Acoustic Phonetics, 2005)

Using the equation: Frequency (Hz) = wave speed (ms^{-1}) / wavelength (m), and assuming that the speed of sound waves in air is 340.29 ms^{-1}, f = v/(4L) where L is the length of the clarinet, or the distance between the mouthpiece and the lowest open hole on the clarinet, since playing different notes changes the length of the pipe and therefore the frequency of the sound.

This formula will produce the note of lowest frequency on the clarinet, which is E3. Changing the length of the pipe by uncovering holes will then produce notes of different frequencies on the lowest register, the chalumeau register. However, the clarinet can also play in other registers when the speaker key is used (Holloway, 2006). This means that the notes are on a higher harmonic as the fundamental frequency is disrupted so the instrument cannot drop down to its bottom register (Nave). An additional hole on the side of the instrument opens up, which forces the air column up to its next resonance; the third harmonic. This is because the hole produces a pressure node at a point where the pressure normally varies for the first harmonic, so the fundamental frequency can no longer be maintained (Nave).

Although the clarinet technically has two open ends, one of which the player blows air through, for the purposes of harmonics, it acts as a closed pipe (Holloway, 2006). This means that it can only play the odd harmonics – notes that start at maximum pressure and end at atmospheric pressure (Wolfe, 2002).

If the wavelength of a note on the chalumeau register is 4L, or four times the length between the mouthpiece and the lowest open key, then a note with the same fingering but played on the clarino register should have a wavelength of $\frac{4}{3}$L (Holloway, 2006). The wavelength value is the distance between the original point on the sine curve where the pressure is at a maximum to each later point where the pressure equals zero. There are now three pressure nodes instead of 1 in the length of the clarinet, making the wavelength $\frac{4}{3}$L. Similarly, a note with the same fingering played on the altissimo register should have a wavelength of $\frac{4}{5}$L.

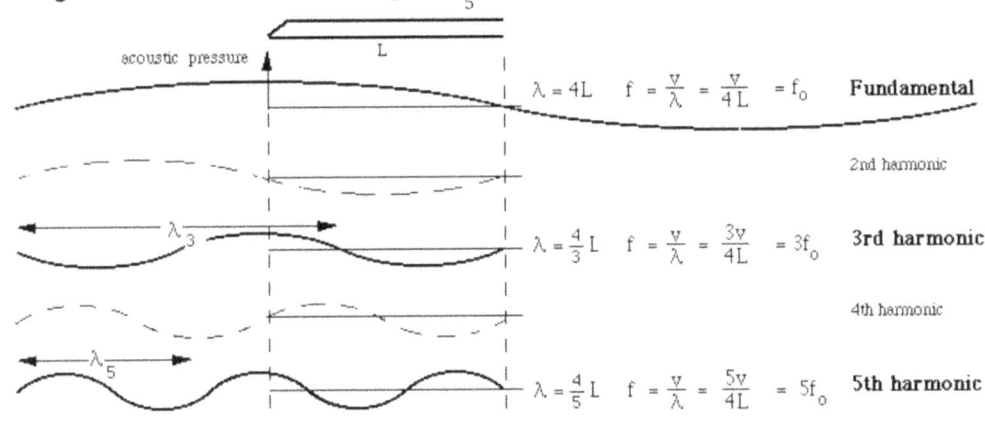

(Wolfe, 2002)

I wanted to prove this idea through experimentation with my clarinet, using the relationship $v = f\lambda$ to compare my own results for the wavelength of notes at a particular frequency with the accepted value for the speed of sound.

Variables

Dependent: Distance between key and mouthpiece
Independent: Frequency of note produced
Controls:

- The clarinet used, as different models can have different lengths between keys, or the wood could have different expansive properties, also altering the length
- Surrounding conditions, as far as possible in order to prevent expansion of the clarinet and resultant changes in frequency recordings (e.g. carrying out the experiments in the same place, at the same time of day)

Hypothesis

The length between the mouthpiece and the hole will be $\frac{1}{4}\lambda$ for the notes tested on the chalumeau register, $\frac{3}{4}\lambda$ for the notes on the clarino register and $\frac{5}{4}\lambda$ for the notes on the altissimo register. I will be able to see if my results are accurate by plotting them on a scatter graph; the speed of sound will be the gradient, and the closer this is to the accepted value of 340.29 ms^{-1}, the greater the accuracy.

Equipment

- Frequency sensor
- Clarinet
- Tape measure

Method

1. Play note and record frequency using frequency sensor
2. Repeat for a variety of notes over the three different registers
3. Measure the distance between the top of the mouthpiece and the top of the hole below the lowest covered one
4. Repeat for all six main holes on the instrument
5. Calculate the wavelength for each frequency by multiplying the measured length by 4 for the chalumeau register, $\frac{4}{3}$ for the clarino register and $\frac{4}{5}$ for the altissimo register.
6. Calculate the wavelength for each frequency using the formula v = fλ.

Results

Chalumeau register

Note Name	Frequency (Hz) ± 0.01 Hz	Measured length (m) ± 0.005m	Wavelength (m)	Wavelength (m) calculated using v = fλ
G3	172.26	0.470	1.88	1.98
A3	193.79	0.410	1.64	1.76
B3	215.33	0.390	1.56	1.58
C4	236.86	0.360	1.44	1.44
D4	258.39	0.290	1.16	1.32
E4	301.46	0.270	1.08	1.13

Clarino register

Note Name	Frequency (Hz) ± 0.01 Hz	Measured length (m)	Wavelength (m)	Wavelength (m) calculated using v = fλ
D5	516.79	0.470	0.627	0.658
E5	581.39	0.410	0.547	0.585
F5	624.46	0.390	0.520	0.544
G5	689.06	0.360	0.480	0.494
A5	775.19	0.290	0.387	0.439
B5	882.86	0.270	0.360	0.385

Altissimo register

Note Name	Frequency (Hz) ± 0.01 Hz	Measured length (m)	Wavelength (m)	Wavelength (m) calculated using v = fλ
C#6	990.52	0.410	0.328	0.344
D6	1033.59	0.390	0.312	0.329
E6	1162.79	0.360	0.288	0.293
F6	1270.45	0.360	0.288	0.268
G6	1399.65	0.410	0.328	0.243

Data processing

Chalumeau register

Measured length	Percentage uncertainty in length (%)	Wave-length (m)	Percentage uncertainty in wavelength (%)	Absolute uncertainty in wavelength (m)	1/ wavelength (m)	1/ calculated wavelength (m)
0.470	0.011	1.88	0.044	8.272×10^{-4}	0.532	0.505
0.410	0.012	1.64	0.048	7.872×10^{-4}	0.610	0.568
0.390	0.013	1.56	0.052	8.112×10^{-4}	0.641	0.633
0.360	0.014	1.44	0.056	8.064×10^{-4}	0.694	0.694
0.290	0.017	1.16	0.068	7.888×10^{-4}	0.862	0.758
0.270	0.019	1.08	0.076	8.208×10^{-4}	0.926	0.885

Clarino register

Measured length	Percentage uncertainty in length (%)	Wave-length (m)	Percentage uncertainty in wavelength (%)	Absolute uncertainty in wavelength (m)	1/ wavelength (m)	1/ calculated wavelength (m)
0.470	0.011	0.627	0.015	9.405×10^{-5}	1.59	1.52
0.410	0.012	0.547	0.016	8.752×10^{-5}	1.83	1.71
0.390	0.013	0.520	0.017	8.840×10^{-5}	1.92	1.84
0.360	0.014	0.480	0.019	9.120×10^{-5}	2.08	2.02
0.290	0.017	0.387	0.023	8.901×10^{-5}	2.58	2.28
0.270	0.019	0.360	0.025	9.000×10^{-5}	2.78	2.60

Altissimo register

Measured length	Percentage uncertainty in length (%)	Wave-length (m)	Percentage uncertainty in wavelength (%)	Absolute uncertainty in wavelength (m)	1/ wavelength (m)	1/ calculated wavelength (m)
0.410	0.012	0.328	0.0096	3.149×10^{-5}	3.05	2.91
0.390	0.013	0.312	0.0104	3.245×10^{-5}	3.21	3.04
0.360	0.014	0.288	0.0112	3.226×10^{-5}	3.47	3.41
0.360	0.014	0.288	0.0112	3.226×10^{-5}	3.47	3.73
0.410	0.012	0.328	0.0096	3.149×10^{-5}	3.05	4.12

Graphs

Using the equation v = fλ, I have plotted the measured wavelengths for each register in order to compare them with the calculated wavelengths, which demonstrate an accurate value of the frequency.

To check whether my results are accurate, I will rearrange the equation v = fλ so that the speed of sound is the gradient.

v = fλ

$f = \frac{v}{\lambda}$

$f = v \times \frac{1}{\lambda}$

y = mx + c

The uncertainties that I calculated for this set of experiments were very small, which is why they are not particularly visible on the graphs.

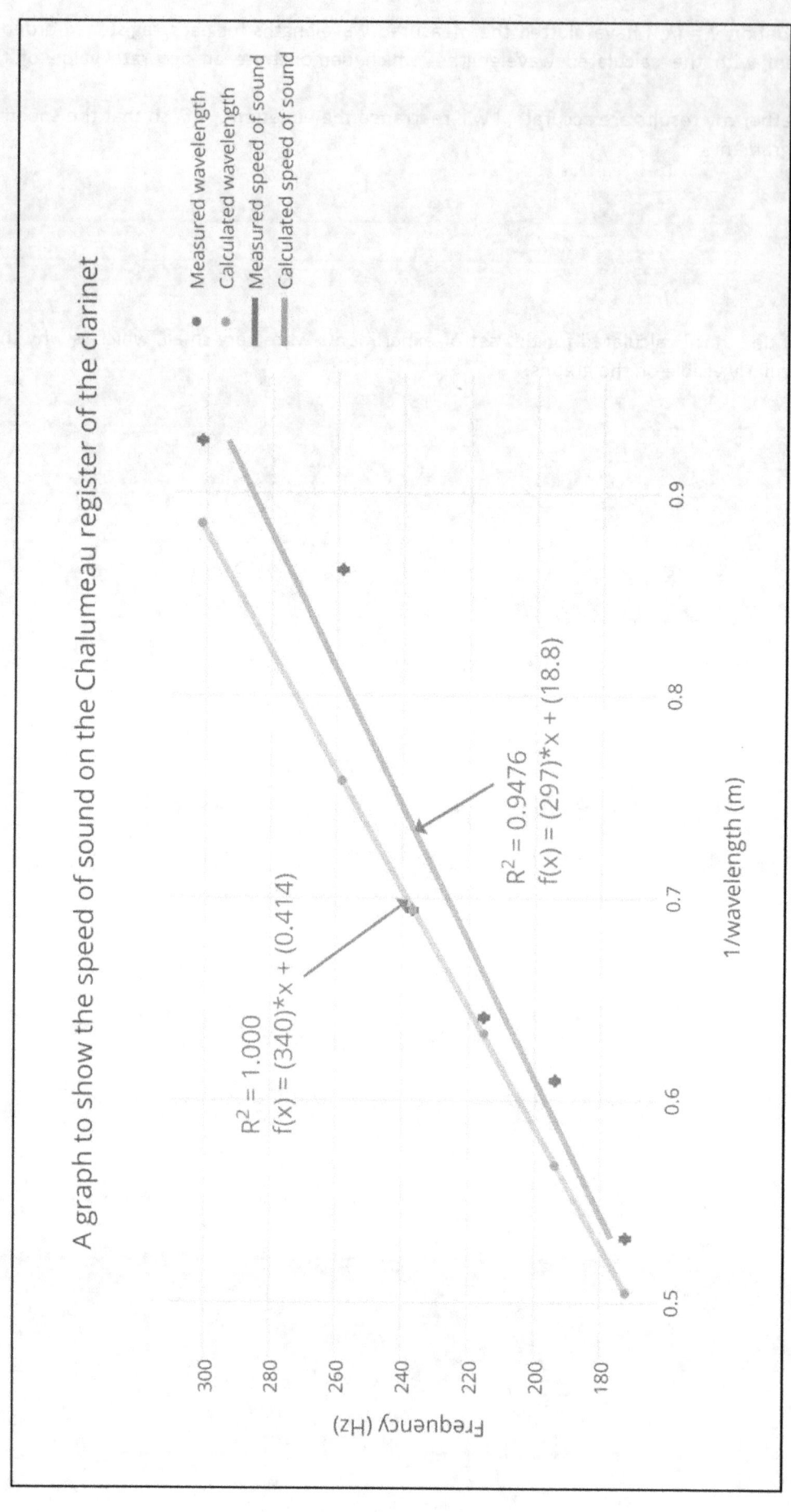

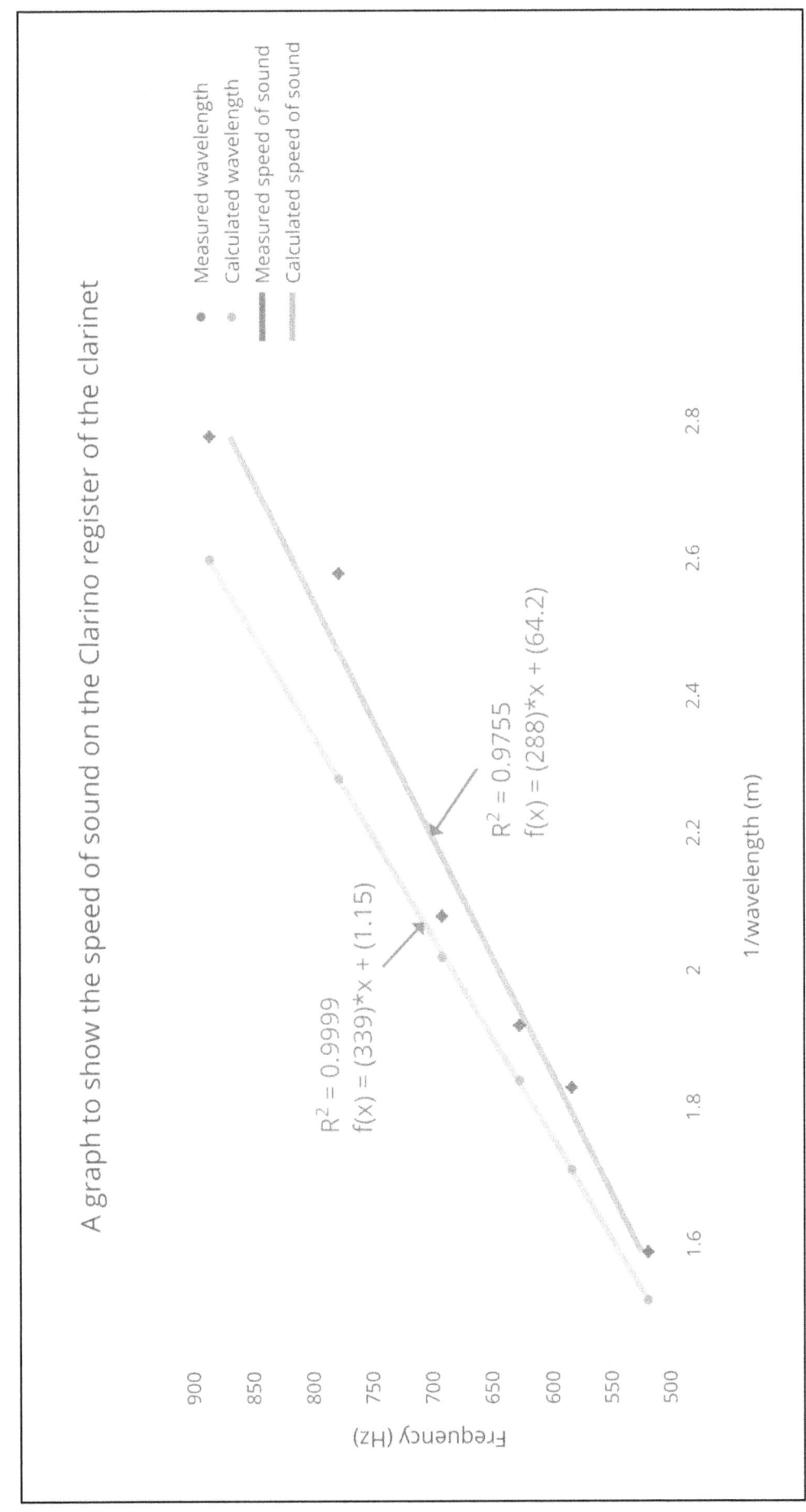

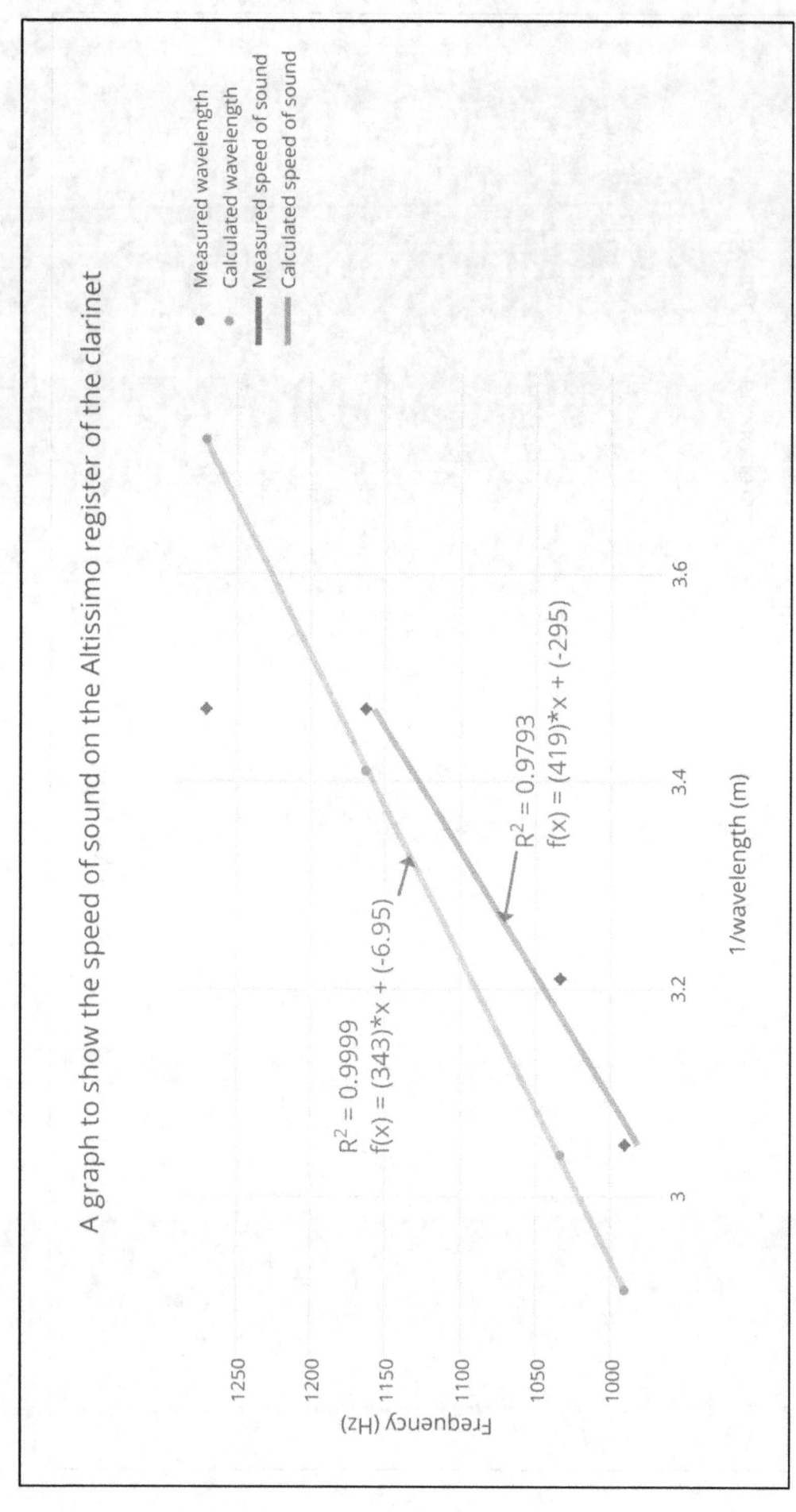

Conclusion

The graphs prove my hypothesis to be correct to some extent. Using the results for which L, or the length between the clarinet mouthpiece and the lowest open tone hole, had been multiplied by 4, I found the gradient of the graph, and hence the speed of sound, to be 297 ms^{-1} for the chalumeau register, which is below the expected value of approximately 340 ms^{-1}. However, the graph shows a linear relationship which would have been directly proportional had it not been affected by systematic error. For the value of the gradient to have fitted into the v = fλ equation, the line of best fit would have passed through the origin. Nevertheless, my calculated value of the gradient was fairly close to the expected value, and probably would have improved in accuracy along with improvements to my experiment procedure.

For the clarino register, where my values of L were multiplied by $\frac{4}{3}$, I calculated the speed of sound inside the clarinet to be 288 ms^{-1}, which is also slower than expected. However, the line of best fit is also linear and the variables are close to being directly proportional, indicating that the predicted relationship between frequency and wavelength is correct, but that the experiment was subject to large amounts of error.

Using the values of L that were multiplied by $\frac{4}{5}$, I calculated the speed of sound to be 419 ms^{-1} for the altissimo register. I removed my last result from the third graph as it was anomalous and made it difficult to draw an accurate line of best fit. The value that I calculated is larger than the accepted value for the speed of sound, and the relationship between the data points is not as linear or as close to being directly proportional as for the other registers. However, 419 ms^{-1} is still relatively close to 340 ms^{-1}.

Evaluation

The clarinet is not a perfectly uniform cylindrical pipe but the experiment assumes that it is. It was also assumed that the wave finishes at the first open tone hole, but it actually extends somewhat beyond this hole; this is known as an end effect (Wolfe, 2002). This means that the calculated wavelengths may have been under the value of the true wavelength, which explains why the wavelengths represented by the red points are frequently lower than those represented by the blue points. To reduce this error, I could have accounted for the end effect by adding 3 cm onto each of my results. This would have provided a more directly proportional linear relationship for my graph.

It was difficult to measure the length between the mouthpiece and holes accurately, due to the bumpy structure of the instrument and the lips of some of the holes changing the actual covered length of the pipe, which I found hard to take into account. My results tended to be to the nearest centimetre because it was too difficult to see if any millimetre divisions should be taken into account. This may have caused random human error in measurements of length. To reduce this error, I could perhaps have compared my measurements with measurements of the clarinet from a database and calculated an average.

It was difficult to measure the frequency of the notes in the altissimo register. This could have been because the register key was being used, so the frequency meter sometimes picked up the frequency of the lower note, with the same fingering, that would have been played had the register key not been pressed down.

Furthermore, measuring the length from the mouthpiece to the lowest open tone hole on the instrument was less simple when dealing with the altissimo register, because alternating open and closed tone holes are often required to produce the note, rather than consecutive closed holes. This explains why the results for the altissimo register are not as expected, and why I had to miss out an anomalous result from the graph.

Subtle changes in environment such as the temperature of room could have influenced the temperature of the wood that makes up the clarinet, causing expansion and therefore altering the recorded frequency. Nevertheless, the frequency sensor tended to settle at the same value for recorded frequencies, but I think that there should have been some variation between readings for the same note. This was a systematic error with the equipment that I used, which may have impacted the precision of my results. In order to obtain more precise data, I could have sourced a more responsive frequency sensor and compared results from this to my original ones.

Results were taken by the same person playing the clarinet, which could have led to inaccuracies in the readings, although it is doubtful whether this would be a problem. To reduce the chance of human error, the experiment could be carried out with two people; one clarinettist and one recorder of results.

Part 2: The effect of temperature on the clarinet

Having proven that the clarinet operates as a closed pipe with standing waves, I wanted to further investigate the effect that temperature has on the frequency of the notes.

Variables

Independent: the temperature of the air inside the mouthpiece
Dependent: the frequency of the note produced by the mouthpiece
Control variables:
- The mouthpiece, reed and ligature used, as different mouthpiece shapes and reed thicknesses could also have an impact on the frequency of the note
- The acclimatisation time for the mouthpiece in the incubator

Hypothesis

As the mouthpiece is incubated at higher temperatures, the temperature of the air molecules inside should increase. This means that their kinetic energy and thus their speed will also rise (Gale, 2010). Referring to the equation $v = f\lambda$, an increased molecule speed for the same wavelength (the constant length of the clarinet mouthpiece) should result in an increased frequency for each measured temperature.

Equipment

- Incubators at temperatures of: 1°C, 22°C, 33°C, 37°C, 45°C, 57°C
- Thermometer
- Clarinet mouthpiece with ligature and reed attached
- Stopclock
- Recording device
- Audacity web software

Method

1. Incubate mouthpiece and reed for a period of ten minutes at 3°C
2. Remove mouthpiece from incubator and record the note produced
3. Incubate twice more for ten minute, blowing the mouthpiece again and recording the note at the end of each incubation
4. Repeat the procedure for incubator temperatures at five additional values
5. Input the recordings into Audacity and select a 1 second clip
6. Use the frequency trace function to work out the average frequency of the note, looking at the first, third, fifth and seventh peaks

Example of clipping of note and frequency spectrum for this note:

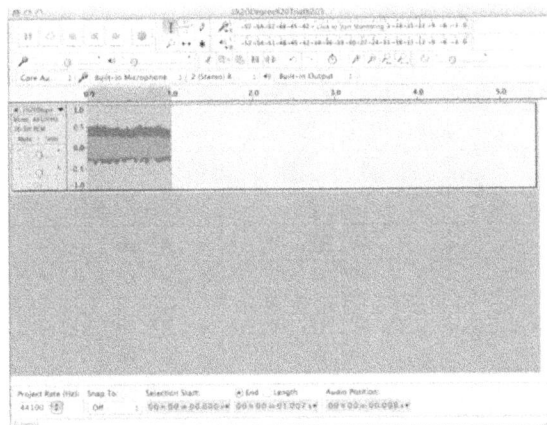
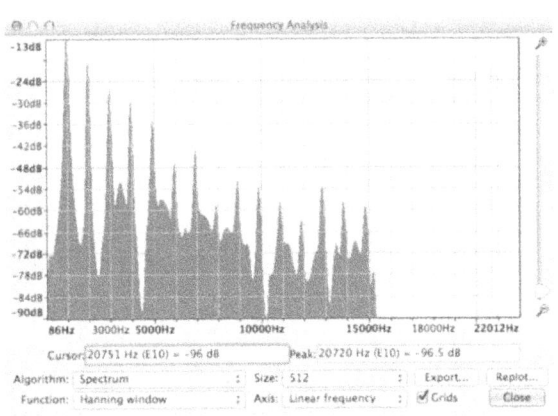

Results

Temperature of air inside mouthpiece (°C) ± 0.01 °C	Frequency value at peak on Audacity spectrum plotter (Hz) ± 0.01 Hz											
	Trial 1				Trial 2				Trial 3			
	1	3	5	7	1	3	5	7	1	3	5	7
1	1003	3027	4975	6962	1003	2913	4823	6733	1003	2989	4975	6962
22	1041	3180	5281	7382	1041	3218	5357	7497	1041	3218	5396	7535
33	1041	3218	5319	7420	1041	3218	5319	7458	1041	3142	5243	7344
37	1041	3180	5281	7382	1041	3257	5396	7573	1041	3180	5243	7382
45	1041	3218	5319	7420	1041	3218	5357	7497	1041	3257	5396	7382
57	1117	3257	5434	7649	1117	3295	5434	7573	1041	3180	5281	7382

Data processing

Temperature of air inside mouthpiece (°C) ± 0.01 °C	Uncertainty in frequency (Hz)				Average uncertainty in frequency (Hz)
	1	3	5	7	
1	0.01	57.00	76.00	114.50	62
22	0.01	19.00	57.50	76.50	38
33	0.01	38.00	38.00	57.00	33
37	0.01	38.50	76.50	95.50	53
45	0.01	19.50	38.50	57.50	29
57	38.00	57.50	76.50	133.5	71

Temperature of air inside mouthpiece (°C) ± 0.01 °C	Mean frequency of note recorded on spectrum trace (Hz)			
	Trial 1	Trial 2	Trial 3	Mean
1	3992	3868	3982	3947 ± 62
22	4221	4278	4298	4266 ± 38
33	4250	4259	4193	4234 ± 33
37	4221	4317	4205	4248 ± 53
45	4250	4278	4269	4266 ± 29
57	4364	4355	4221	4313 ± 71

Graph

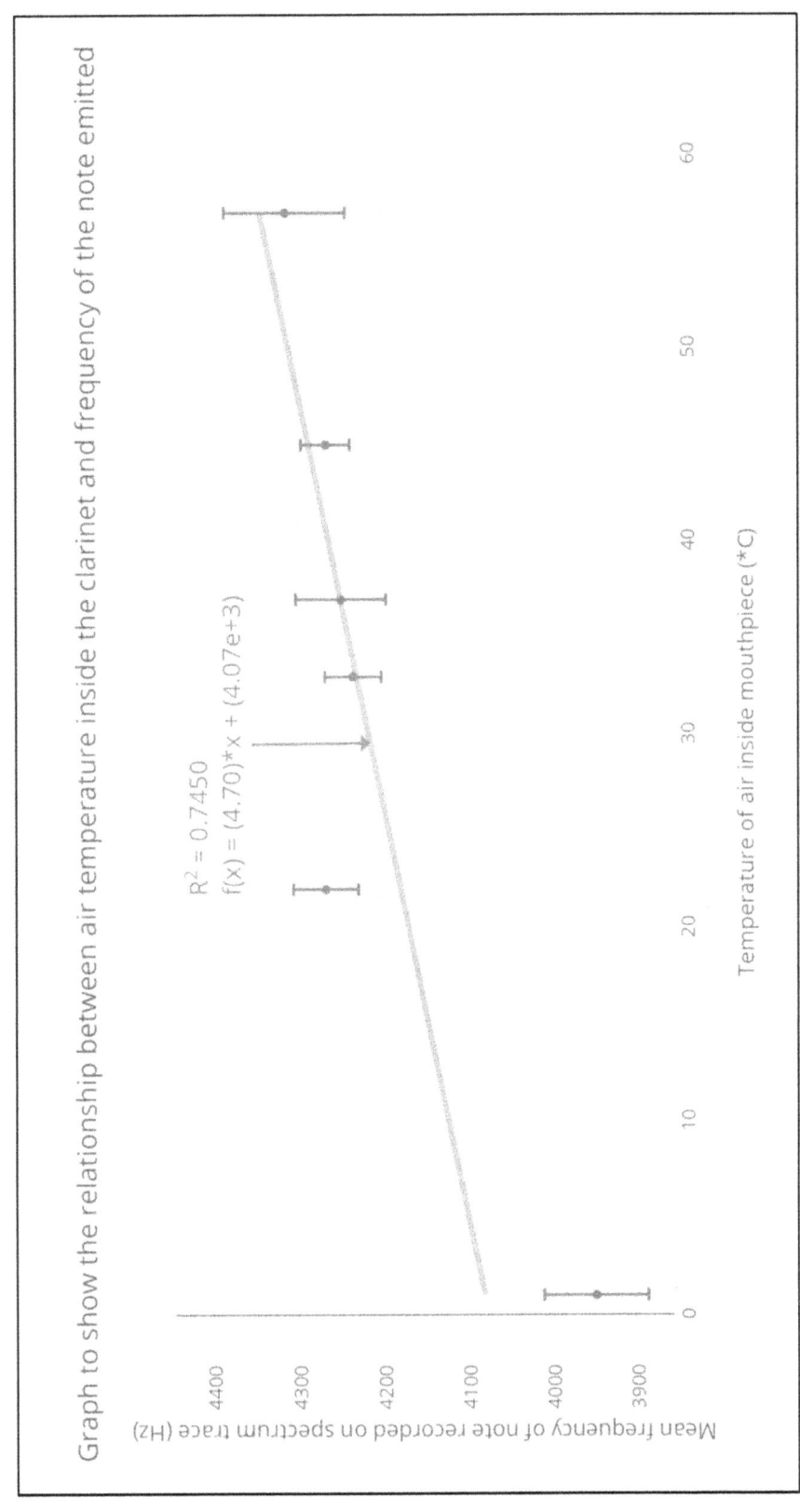

Calculation of maximum and minimum gradients

Best gradient from line of best fit = 4.70

Minimum gradient = (4210 − 4100)/ (50 − 23) = 4.07

Maximum gradient = (4225 − 4000) / (40 − 14) = 8.65

(8.65 − 4.07)/ 2 = 2.29

Gradient = 4.70 Hz °C^{-1} ± 2.29 Hz °C^{-1}

Conclusion

My hypothesis that an increased air temperature inside the clarinet mouthpiece would result in an increased frequency was proven correct to some extent. I calculated an average value of frequency for each air temperature, before plotting this on a graph, and my line of best fit shows a positive correlation between the two factors, indicating that raising the air temperature does result in an increased frequency value for a note of the same pitch (and therefore of the same wavelength). For example, the average value of frequency at a temperature of 1°C was 3947 Hz, whereas the value at 57°C was 4313 Hz. The value of frequency for 22°C was 4266 Hz, which appears as an anomaly on the graph, as it is higher than expected for such a temperature. The relationship between temperature and frequency does not appear to be directly proportional, as the graph does not go through the origin, and many of the data points appear to have been affected by random error that has moved them off the line of best fit. This is also shown by the high uncertainty of ± 2.29 Hz °C^{-1} in the gradient of the line of best fit, which I calculated from my graph.

Evaluation

My graph shows that this experiment was impacted by both random error, which would have affected the precision of my results, and systematic error, which would have affected the accuracy.

It would have been more ideal to be able to use a greater range of incubator temperatures at more regular intervals. However, the temperature of the plastic of the mouthpiece had to be considered so that I did not burn or freeze my lips. Furthermore, the incubators that I used were already at set temperatures, and could only be changed by changing the setting and then recording the temperature reached afterwards. Consequently I did not have much control over the temperatures that I used.

The temperature of the mouthpiece, and thus of the air inside, changed rapidly once removed from the incubator. I had to allow a small amount of time to start the recording device before playing the note, so the air temperature at this time may have been a few degrees different to the recorded temperature. This would have caused systematic error in that it affected all my results, but also random error in that the decrease in temperature would have been greater for a given time when the mouthpiece was at higher temperatures. It would have been difficult to avoid this problem, but involving another person in the experiment, who would take charge of the operating device, might have reduced the error.

The incubation period for the mouthpiece may not have been long enough, which would have made the air temperature inside the mouthpiece subject to systematic error. Perhaps an incubation period of 20 minutes or 30 minutes instead of 10 minutes would have ensured that the recorded temperatures were more precise.

Using the Audacity software to calculate frequency was quite difficult – the readability of the equipment may have resulted in systematic error, because reading off a trace meant that I was not always sure where the peak value lay. I chose to use only the first, third, fifth and seventh peaks from the frequency spectrum, to save time, but my results may have been more accurate had I taken values from all the peaks, as the mean would have been more accurate. This may have eliminated the non-zero intercept on my graph.

I also found it difficult to control the pressure that I was applying to the mouthpiece when I was playing a note without the rest of the clarinet. This could have impacted the pitch, and therefore frequency, of all the notes I played, causing random error and perhaps accounting in part for the anomaly at 22°C on the graph. Taking more repeats and another average of my results could have reduced this error.

I could also have tested the impact of a number of other independent variables on the frequency of the note emitted by the clarinet mouthpiece, such as the thickness of the reed, the distance between the reed and the mouthpiece, or the width of the hole at the end of the mouthpiece. This latter suggestion I could have achieved by wrapping paper of different thicknesses around the inside of the mouthpiece tube.

Bibliography

Acoustic Phonetics. (2005). *Sound Waves*. Available at:
http://home.cc.umanitoba.ca/~krussll/phonetics/acoustic/sound-waves.html (Last Accessed: 16 December 2015)

Gale, B. (2010). *Pitch and Temperature.* Available at: http://www.theconcertband.com/index.php/resources/music-physics/pitch-and-temperature_(Last Accessed: 16 December 2015)

Holloway, C. (2006). *The Physics of the Clarinet.* Available at: http://milankie.huffmancoding.com/Portfolio/cehhphys12.pdf (Last Accessed: 16 December 2015)

Nave, R. *Register Key of Clarinet.* Available at: http://hyperphysics.phy-astr.gsu.edu/hbase/music/clarinet.html (Last Accessed: 16 December 2015)

The Physics Classroom. Pitch and Frequency. Available at: http://www.physicsclassroom.com/class/sound/Lesson-2/Pitch-and-Frequency (Last Accessed: 16 December 2015)

Wolfe, J. (2002). *Clarinet acoustics: an introduction.* Available at: http://newt.phys.unsw.edu.au/jw/clarinetacoustics.html#pipe (Last Accessed: 16 December 2015)

# 7. IS IT MORE ENERGY EFFICIENT TO USE A SMALL PERSONAL FAN OR A LARGER, MULTI-PERSON FAN, FOR PERSONAL COOLING IN A HOT CLIMATE?

Is it more energy efficient to use a small single-person fan or a larger, multi-person fan, for personal cooling in a hot climate?

Introduction

Living in the Bahamas, where it is very hot for a good portion of the year, fans are essential. As we do not use AC in my household, finding a fan which will cool us most efficiently is an almost daily consideration. There has been much debate in my family as to whether a small personal fan or a larger shared fan is more effective and efficient. In addition, I am interested in renewable energy resources and have wondered whether the very large wind turbines, which are often criticised for being unsightly, are the most effective way to produce energy. This exploration will therefore investigate the efficiency of household fans with different turbine sizes at varying electrical inputs and speeds, to answer the question: **Is it more energy efficient to use a small single-person fan or a larger, multi-person fan, for personal cooling in a hot climate?**

We use basically two sizes of cooling fan in our household, a small diametre personal fan (0.185 m), which can only cool one person, and a larger diameter fan (0.45 m) which can cool two people sitting reasonably close together. The efficiency of these two fan sizes will therefore be investigated, by varying the electrical input and measuring the corresponding turbine and air speeds.

The energy efficiency of an electric fan will depend upon the efficiency of the electric motor, in converting electrical energy into the Kinetic Energy (E_k) of the rotating fan blades, and the efficiency of the fan blades in then converting this E_k into E_k of moving air. Therefore, in order to attempt to investigate both factors, both the velocity of the airflow produced and the angular velocity of the fan blades will be measured.

Exploration

Background

Fans create a cooling effect by means of the moving air carrying heat away from the body. This cooling effect was originally assessed as a straightforward rate of heat loss in kcal/m²/hour, and a relationship between air velocity and rate of heat loss was developed giving a wind chill index (Australian Bureau of Meteorology, 2010) as follows:

Wind chill index = $(\sqrt{10V} - V + 10.5)(33 - Ta)$ where V = air velocity and T=temperature

This simplifies to the general form, Wind chill index = $a\sqrt{v} + bv$

So it can be seen that the heat loss is not simply directly proportional to air velocity. Also, when assessing the cooling effect of moving air on human beings it is not only the rate of heat loss that is important, but also human perception of the cooling effect (Australian Bureau of Meteorology, 2010). More recently therefore, a parameter called the chill factor has been developed, which expresses the cooling effect of moving air on the human body, at a given temperature and velocity, by expressing the effect as an equivalent temperature in still air, ie a temperature in still air which "feels" the same to a human being as the moving air. The relationship then, between air velocity and cooling effect, or comfort, is not simple. But since, no matter how it is calculated, the cooling effect always increases with velocity, only air velocity will be considered in this investigation.

Calculating Wind Power output of fan

In order to assess the power output of the fan, in terms of the airflow it produces, the equation for the input power of a wind power generator will be used $1/2 \rho A v^3$. A is the cross-sectional area of the fan turbine, remembering that in these fans there is a large hub at the centre of the blades that does not produce any airflow. Therefore, the shape of the airstream produced is assumed to be a cylinder of diameter equal to the diameter of the fan turbine, with a void, of no airflow, in the centre, of diameter equal to the hub (i.e. an annular prism).

Variables

Independent Variables: Fan turbine diameter, Current and Voltage input
Dependent Variables: Fan turbine angular velocity and velocity of outgoing air
Control Variables: a.) Air density and humidity b.) resistance to fan's outgoing airflow

Variable a.) was controlled by performing the test in an air conditioned room. If the temperature had not been controlled between tests, the angular velocity of the fans would have varied in response, not only to the independent variables, but also the varying air density. Variable b.) was controlled by ensuring that the fans were in the same location in relation to surrounding objects and walls between tests, if this had not been the case then the velocity of the fans outgoing airflow would have changed in response to the differing locations as well as the independent variables.

Key to Symbols Used for variables:
- v : velocity of airflow
- I : current to fan
- V : voltage across fan
- A : effective cross-sectional area of fan turbine
- ω : angular velocity of fan blades
- E_k : Kinetic Energy of airstream produced by fan
- P : Power

Apparatus

- Fan 1: Turbine diameter = 0.45 m diameter, Hub diameter = 0.15 m
- Fan 2: Turbine diameter = 0.185 m diameter, Hub diameter = 0.04 m
- Anemometer ± 0.1 km/h
- Digital Multimeter ± 0.001 Amps, ± 0.1 Volts
- External speed controller with full range control (Variable Resistor)
- Strobe Light ± 1 Hz
- Paint (to mark blades)
- Electrical Wire
- Ruler ± 0.5 mm
- Electrical Connector blocks

NOTE: Each of the fans incorporates its own internal three speed controller, but because this controller allowed only three speeds the external speed controller, with full range control, was used to allow readings anywhere between 0 and maximum speed. Throughout the investigation the fans' internal speed controllers were fixed at the highest speed setting.

Method

1) The circuit shown in Fig. A.1 was assembled first with the small fan. The speed controller (represented as a variable resistor in Fig A.1) was connected into the live side of the fan lead using connector blocks. Care was taken to be consistent in method between repeats of this process as variation could have an effect on the resistance of the circuit and therefore the results. The digital multimeter (represented as an ammeter and a voltmeter in Fig .1) was also connected into the circuit.
2) The current and voltage to the fan were adjusted by varying the setting on the speed controller and at each setting the current and voltage were recorded. Because only one digital multimeter was available each setting had to be repeated, once with it connected as an ammeter and once as a voltmeter.
3) At each setting, the velocity of the fan's airflow was recorded, by placing the anemometer at the same location and distance (0.3m) from the fan.
4) At each setting, the strobe light was set at a very high frequency and directed at the fan (with the lights switched off and the curtains closed). The frequency was then steadily reduced until the fan blades appeared to stop moving. The frequency was recorded. This method of reducing the frequency from a high level was used to ensure that when the blades first appeared stationary, one rotation of the blade was taking place for each flash of the strobe, not multiple rotations. Also one blade of the fan was distinguished with paint to ensure that when the motion of the fan appeared stationary, a full rotation of the fan was taking place for each flash, not a partial rotation.
5) The air velocity was also recorded without the speed controller in the circuit. This is to assess whether the speed controller itself was effecting the electrical supply in any way when it was at maximum velocity setting.

6) The whole process was then repeated using the large fan.

Safety Procedure:

Before any of the adaptations were made to the electrical components or circuitry, all items were disconnected from the power source. Additionally, it was ensured that there was no history of epilepsy or similar conditions before the strobe light was used.

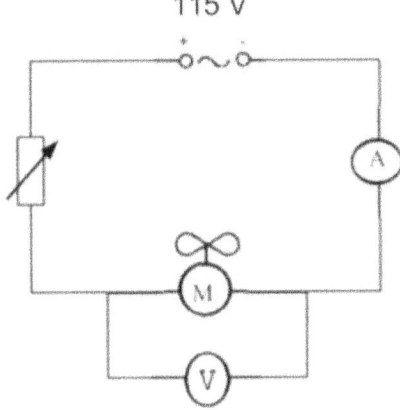

Figure A.1: Circuit diagram of set up used in experiment

Results

Raw Data

Table 1.: Small Fan

Voltage across fan (Volts) ± 0.1 V	Current Through Circuit (Amps) ± 0.001 A	Air Velocity (ms^{-1}) ± 0.03	Strobe flashes in Hertz ± 1 Hz
115	0.429	4.06	36
111	0.399	3.94	35
93.8	0.377	3.50	33
106	0.355	2.50	31
98.0	0.305	1.72	25
88.6	0.266	1.67	20
82.6	0.231	1.17	17
70.4	0.207	0.690	11

Table 2.: *Big Fan*

Voltage Across Fan (Volts) ± 0.1 V	Current Through Circuit (Amps) ± 0.001 A	Air Velocity (ms^{-1}) ± 0.03	Strobe flashes in Hertz ± 1 Hz
124	0.730	4.89	18
108	0.640	4.50	17
101	0.575	4.31	16
89.5	0.495	4.03	14
73.0	0.419	3.25	11
65.1	0.344	2.28	9
50.0	0.312	1.80	7
55.9	0.277	1.28	5

Example Calculations for Tables 1 and 2 (using first data set in Table 1):

Conversion of Air Velocity

14.6 kmh^{-1}
$\Rightarrow$ Velocity in m = (14.6 x 1000) ÷ 3600
    = 4.06 ms^{-1}

Conversion of Air Velocity Error

0.1 kmh^{-1} = 0.03 ms^{-1}

Derived Results

Table 3.: *Small Fan*

Electric Power Input (Watts)		Wind Power Output (Watts)		Angular Velocity in rad s^{-1} ± 6 rad s^{-1}	System Efficiency (%)	
49.4	± 0.3 %	1.05	± 10%	226	2.10	± 10%
44.3	± 0.3%	0.960	± 10%	220	2.20	± 10%
35.4	± 0.4%	0.672	± 10%	207	1.90	± 10%
37.6	± 0.4%	0.344	± 10%	195	0.910	± 10%
29.9	± 0.4%	0.145	± 10%	157	0.340	± 10%
23.6	± 0.5%	0.073	± 10%	126	0.310	± 10%
19.0	± 0.6%	0.025	± 10%	107	0.100	± 20%
14.6	± 0.6%	0.00520	± 20%	69.0	0.0400	± 20%

Table 4.: *Big Fan*

Electric Power Input (Watts)		Wind Power Output (Watts)		Angular Velocity in rad s^{-1} ± 6 rad s^{-1}	System Efficiency (%)	
90.5	± 0.2%	5.05	± 6%	113	5.58	± 6%
69.3	± 0.2%	3.94	± 6%	107	5.68	± 6%
58.2	± 0.3%	3.45	± 6%	101	5.93	± 6%
44.3	± 0.3%	2.82	± 6%	88.0	6.37	± 7%
30.6	± 0.4%	1.48	± 7%	69.0	4.84	± 7%
22.4	± 0.4%	0.510	± 8%	57.0	2.28	± 8%
15.6	± 0.5%	0.250	± 9%	45.0	1.60	± 9%
15.5	± 0.5%	0.0900	± 10%	32.0	0.580	± 10%

Example Calculations for Tables 3 and 4 (using first data set in Table 3):
Electric Power Input:

Power = Current x Voltage
P = IV
P = 115 x 0.429
P = 49.4 W

Calculating Error for Power Input

In order to find the error the percentage errors are added
Example: First reading for small fan

Percentage Error of P = % error of I + % error of V
$\qquad\qquad\qquad$ = (0.001 ÷ 0.429) x 100 + (0.1 ÷ 115) x 100
$\qquad\qquad\qquad$ = 0.0868% + 0.2331%
$\qquad\qquad\qquad$ = ± 0.3199%
$\qquad\qquad\qquad$ = ± 0.3%

Angular Velocity
ω = strobe flashes x 2π
$\quad$ = 36 x 2π
$\quad$ = 226 rad s^{-1}

Wind Power Output:

Volume of air = Area of turbine x velocity of air
(keeping in mind that the turbine's area does not include the centre hub of the fan as this part does not push out air)

⇒ Where r_1 = the total radius of the fan and r_2 = the radius of the hub
Volume = v ($\pi r_1^2 - \pi r_2^2$)

mass of air (m) = Volume x density
m = Vρ
⇒ m = Vρ($\pi r_1^2 - \pi r_2^2$) 2

E_k = ½ mv^2

$$\Rightarrow E_k = \tfrac{1}{2} \times V\rho(\pi r_1^2 - \pi r_2^2) \times v^2$$
$$= \tfrac{1}{2} A\rho v^3$$

Power = Energy ÷ time
P = E/t
In this case t = 1
$$\Rightarrow P = \tfrac{1}{2} v^3 \rho (\pi r_1^2 - \pi r_2^2)$$

This formula was used to find the power output of both fans at each reading
(Note: the density of air (ρ) = 1.225 kgm^{-3} was used)

$$\Rightarrow P = \tfrac{1}{2} \times (4.06)^3 \times 1.225 \times (\pi(0.0925)^2 - \pi(0.02)^2)$$
$$= 1.05 \text{ Watts}$$

Calculating Error for Power Output
$P = \tfrac{1}{2} A\rho v^3$
The percentage error in P = 3 x percentage error in v + percentage error in A - **Equation 1** (errors in ρ are ignored as it is a standard quantity)
But A itself is a composite quantity, A = $(\pi r_1^2 - \pi r_2^2)$ = 0.0256 m^2
Absolute Error in A is found from, absolute error in r_1^2 + absolute error in r_2^2 - **Equation 2**
Example: Area of small fan
Absolute error on r_1 = 0.0005 m $\Rightarrow$ % error of r_1 = (0.0005 ÷ 0.0925) x 100 = 0.541 %
Absolute error on r_2 = 0.0005 m $\Rightarrow$ % error r_2 = (0.0005 ÷ 0.02) x 100 = 2.5%
$\Rightarrow$ % error of r_1^2 = 2 x 0.541 = 1.082%
    % error of r_2^2 = 2 x 2.5 = 5%
$\Rightarrow$ from **Equation 2**,   Absolute error in A = (0.01082 x 0.0925) + (0.05 x 0.02) = 0.002 m^2
$\Rightarrow$ % error in A = 0.002 ÷ 0.0256 x 100 = 7.81% This is a fixed percentage error for every reading with this fan.
By the same method, the large fan has a fixed percentage error in A of 4%.

Example: First calculation for small fan
From **Equation 1**
% error of P = 3 x % error of v + 7.81% = 300 (0.0277 ÷ 4.06) + 7.81 = 9.86% = 10%

Calculating System Efficiency

Efficiency = $\dfrac{\text{Wind Power Output}}{\text{Electric Power Input}}$ x 100

= 1.05 ÷ 49.4 x 100
= 2%

Calculation of Error in System Efficiency

% Error of Efficiency = % error of output + % error of input
= 0.320 + 9.86
= 10 %
(Bowen, Homer, 2014.)

Figure A.1: Small Fan, Air velocity v Angular Velocity

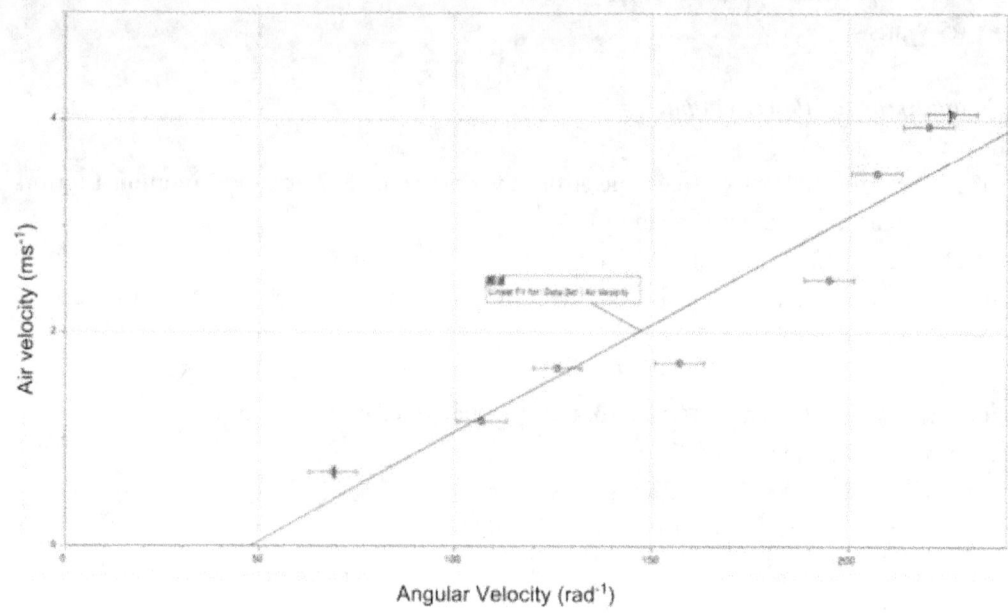

Figure A.2: Big Fan, Air velocity v Angular Velocity

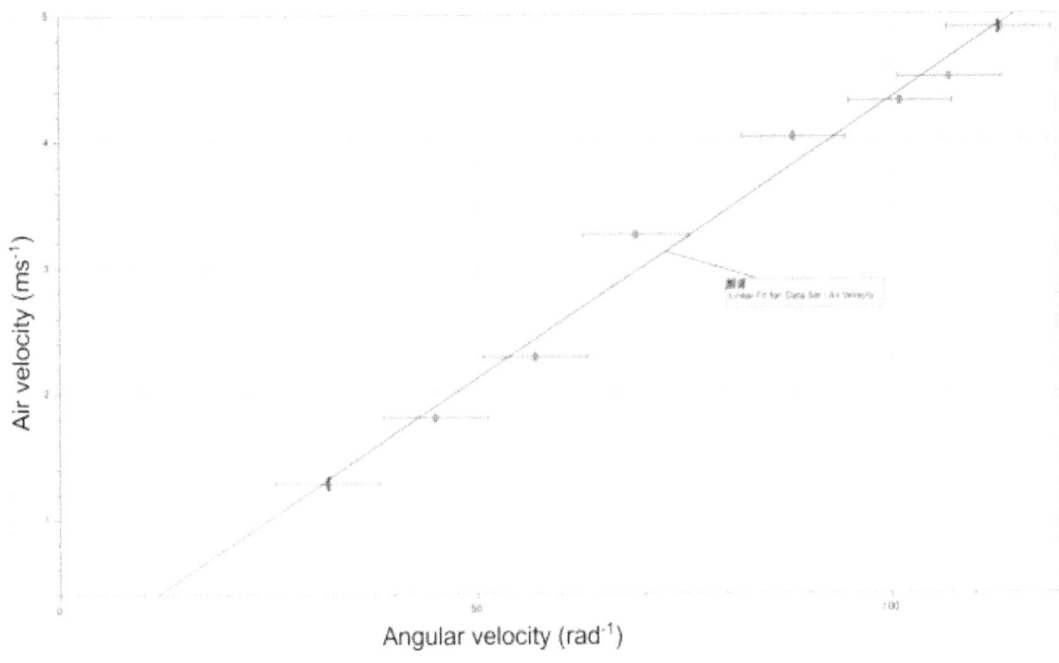

Figure A. 3: Small Fan, Efficiency against Angular Velocity

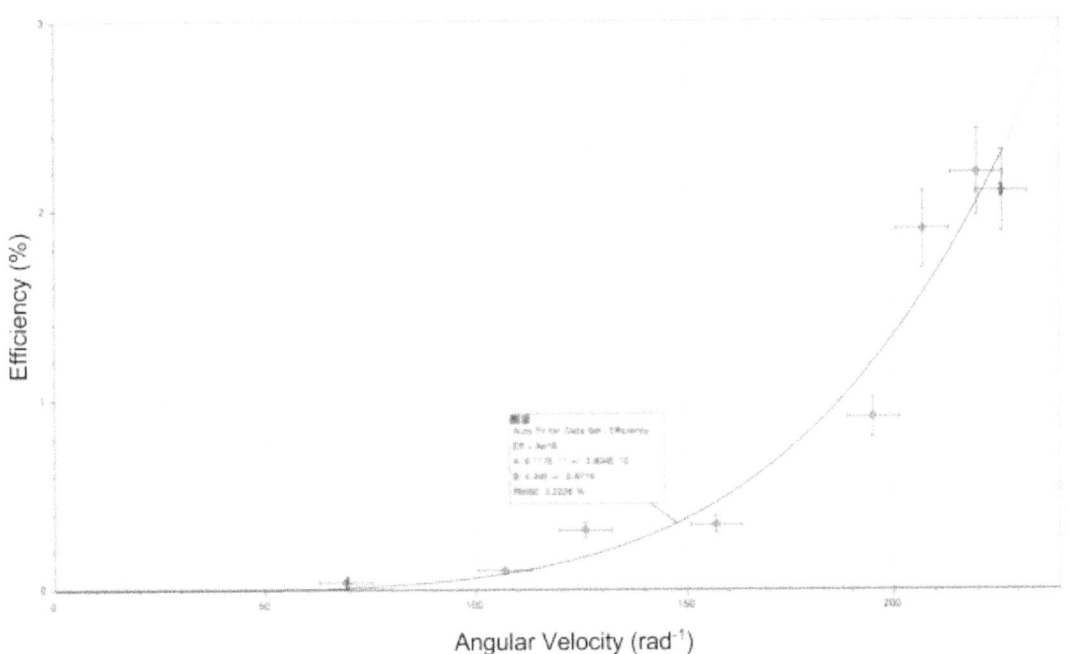

Figure A. 4: Big Fan, Efficiency against Angular Velocity

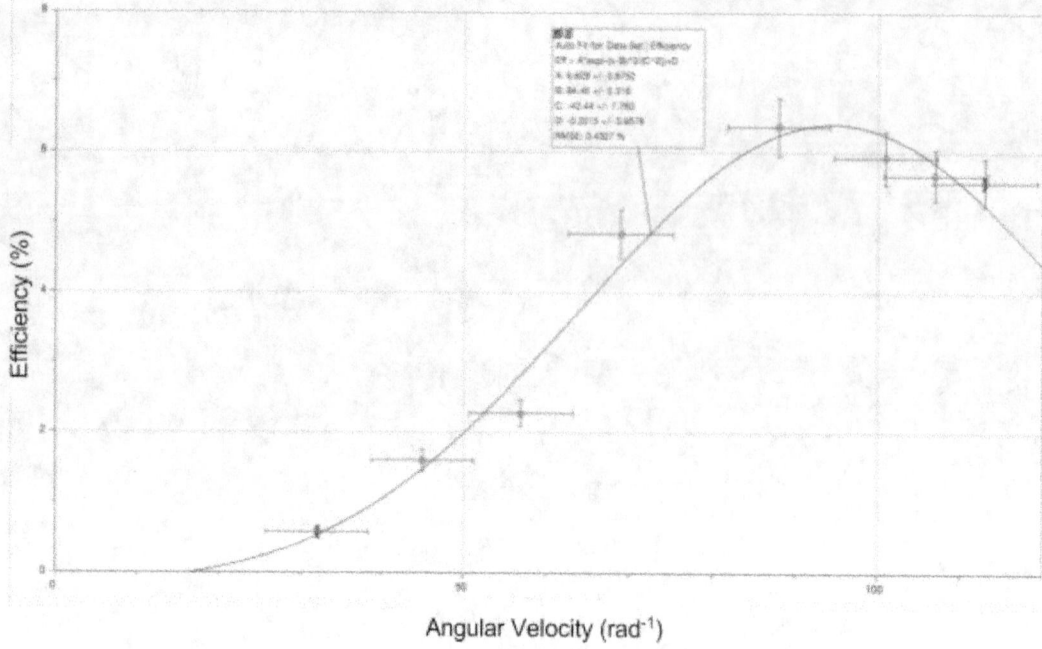

The plots of the fans' output air velocity against angular velocity showed a linear proportionality as might be expected. However, the best fit straight line plots did not pass through the origin, as they should, due to anomalous readings and/or insufficient readings taken close to the origin. This could be rectified by taking more readings at low angular velocities which could identify a different trend in this area. Also, the plot of air velocity against angular velocity for the small fan does not show a peak in the air velocity, but it seems unlikely that it would increase exponentially without reaching a peak. This limitation could be as a result of a lack of readings at the high end of the angular velocities and could be rectified by taking more readings or that the peak is beyond the range of the readigs.

The calculations of the fans' efficiencies showed that the large fan was at least twice as efficient as the small fan at all angular velocities. The plots of efficiency against angular velocity showed that both fans had their highest efficiency at or close to their maximum speed and the efficiency dropped away rapidly if the fan speed were reduced.

A limitation of the study was indicated by the surprisingly low efficiencies that were calculated. It was conjectured that perhaps all the output energy had not been accounted for and therefore some additional investigation was performed. An attempt was made to measure air velocity outside the predicted, annular cross section of the airflow. This was done on the basis that perhaps the turbine was somehow producing an airflow with a diameter larger than that of the turbine. However, when air velocity measurements were taken very close to the fan but outside the predicted airflow diameter, and within the hub diameter, this was found not to be the case. Secondly some air velocity measurements were therefore taken as close to the front of the fans as possible (rather than the 0.3m, as previously used) and here the velocities were found to be higher. In order therefore, to get more accurate results the investigation could be repeated, taking all the air velocities as close to the fans as possible. This would raise all the efficiencies of both fans but would probably not change the comparison between the results, or the conclusions reached, because all the velocities would probably be increased by the same proportion.

The methodology would be improved by taking the measurements of the air velocity closer to the fans. Additionally, as previously stated, only one multimeter was used in this experiment, the introduction of a second multimeter in order to measure the current and voltage simultaneously, would be a significant improvement to the methodology.

Conclusion:

The answer to the original question **Is it more energy efficient to use a small personal fan or a larger, multi-person fan, for personal cooling in a hot climate?** is clear. The large fan is much more energy efficient at all angular velocities and at its maximum efficiency, the large fan produces 4.8 times as much energy output for an input of only 1.8 times. Therefore not only is less energy per person used to cool two people with the big fan but they are cooled much more effectively. And, if the large fan is used for three people, as it can be when sitting side by side to watch, TV for example, then only 61% of the energy is needed with the large fan and the cooling is still 60% more effective.

However, another interesting conclusion can be drawn by looking at the efficiency graphs. Living in the Bahamas it is necessary to have a fan almost all year round but in the cooler months the fan is often put on a lower setting because at lower ambient temperatures the velocity of the air from the fan does not need to be as high, because the required cooling effect is less. It is seen from the graphs that both fans are most efficient at close to their highest speeds, meaning that in a climate where a fan would be needed for varying cooling effects it would be most efficient to have multiple fans with varying maximum velocities which suited each need. This is so that the fan being used is always running at its maximum velocity and therefore efficiency, while still creating the appropriate cooling effect.

Also, the graphs of air velocity versus angular velocity show a direct proportional relationship, indicating that aerodynamic efficiency of the fan turbine is not changing with speed. Therefore, the loss in efficiency at lower fan speeds must be due to electrical factors.

The conclusions reached in this investigation may have been different if cooling fans with different turbine designs were investigated. This would be an interesting extension to the investigation.

Works Cited

Homer, D., Bowen, M. (2014). *Oxford IB Diploma Programme: Physics Course Companion*. Oxford University Press.

Thermal Comfort observations. (2010, February 5). Retrieved March 10, 2017, from http://www.bom.gov.au/info/thermal_stress/#atapproximation

www.ingramcontent.com/pod-product-compliance
Lightning Source LLC
Chambersburg PA
CBHW081101070526
44583CB00018B/2509